SERIOUS ABOUT LEARNING FRENCH.

BY IAN CARROLL.

For Niamh,

my wonderful niece.

Le monde attendes-toi.

Copyright Ian Carroll 2015. All rights for all territories reserved solely by the author.

FOREWORD.

Are you serious about learning French? If so, this book is for you. I have studied French at school, college, university, night school, at language school in Nice, and at an informal conversation club. I have also taught Beginners French for twelve months, read lots of books, listened to countless hours of audio and, guess what? I don't speak French! Okay, un peu. I have a good grasp of the basics and, given the right amount of effort, I know that I could push on leaps and bounds in a short space of time. So what am I doing writing a book about learning French? Well, in all the ways that I have tried to learn French, from the many hours of study, listening to CDs in the car, and all the avenues I've explored to try and learn the language, there have been many things that I wish I had been told. These are the things that I taught my Beginners group, and it is these handy tips and sound advice that I wish to share with you. There are many books on the market that claim to teach you French in a week, a month, or a year. These books often fall into two categories. Either they are a motivational tool to get you fired up, but have little practical merit to actually help you achieve your goal. Or, they are practical manuals that actually de-motivate you because they are overly-academic (great if you're a swot, but not so great for the vast majority who aren't and just want to learn French). My book is going to offer you a real helping hand in learning the language, and will also help to motivate you to undertake the journey ahead. Quite simply, if you are serious about learning French, there can be no better companion piece, however you are planning on reaching your goal, whether that be through books, CDs, a language course, or any of the many ways that you may choose to go about it. This book is based on the many hours that I have spent either learning, teaching, or merely scratching my head in frustration as I've sought to acquire a foothold into the French language. Serious about learning French? Me too. Allez. Let's go.

INTRODUCTION.

It seems to me that learning a language is a huge endeavour, like climbing a mountain or sailing an ocean. It is not to be undertaken lightly, and requires an extraordinary amount of effort. And here's the hard part. No one can climb the mountain for you. The work is going to be all your own. Only by putting one foot in front of the other, by pushing on up, overcoming obstacles and difficulties, can you ever hope to reach the top. Maybe you only want to reach Everest Base Camp, or some mid-point along the way, or maybe you want to get as high as you can go. Whatever your goal, this book can help you.

If you like the analogy of climbing a mountain, then this book is your guide. If you prefer the example of crossing an ocean, then this book is your GPS. The tips and insights given along the way will be your anchor points. You'll get plenty of sustenance and encouragement, and I'll provide the ropes and all the right equipment for your expedition. You may read the book and never leave home. If so, you'll still have had a good look at the top of the mountain, because within these pages you will get an overview of the journey that lies ahead. More importantly though, it is my aim to inspire you to keep moving forward, one step at a time, higher and higher until you reach your goal.

As I have said, I don't speak French. I am nowhere near the level that I have set myself, yet I have circled the base of the mountain a couple of times, and I have looked up. I have solid foundations, and the building blocks to ascend quickly, whenever life affords me the opportunity to do so. I have a real passion for the language, and the ability to inspire others. My Beginners group, who barely spoke a word of French between them, within six months were saying complex two phrase sentences (I am going to go to France and I am going to build a boat, etc). They were able to do this, not through paraphrasing but by being given a good grounding in the language, solid building blocks that they could utilise of their own accord, never being lost, and always being challenged.

This book contains the teaching methods that I employed with the group, and also the things that I learned myself in the many environments I have stepped into in order to learn French. Some are tips handed down by some of the greatest of language teachers, and others are things that I wish I had been told in these classes or other outlets of study. Sometimes, when I'd pass on these tips to others, they would ask me 'Why doesn't anyone ever tell you that?' The answer is, I don't know. Some of the ideas seem obvious. Some not so. I certainly believe that you'll find enough of them here to help you on your way. Like I say, no one can climb the mountain for you, but I can certainly help. Assuming you've read this far, I guess you and I share the same passion for the language and the same desire to improve your language skills. So, what are we waiting for? Let's start climbing. And don't forget your GPS, because you really don't want to make the journey without this (guide) book!

CROSSING THE FIRST HURDLE.

I first started learning French at school. At an open day, the teacher told my parents that I had the best French accent of any pupil that she had ever taught. The only problem was, I didn't know what I was saying! I had an innate ability for how the language should be spoken (maybe it's the writer's ear for dialogue), now all I needed was a vocabulary to go with it. The problem for me was the way that the language was taught. All I can remember about French at school was the introduction to it, which consisted of learning the verbs Avoir, Être, and Aller. As these verbs were conjugated on the blackboard in front of me (note for younger readers, blackboards are what we used to use in schools before computers!), I can remember thinking 'If this is the introduction, then French is going to be impossible', because it was really hard. There was no symmetry or synergy between the three verbs. Each of them had their own unique form, and if this was the beginning of the language, then I thought the rest of it was going to be equally difficult and would probably take a lifetime to master. Straight away, I gave up. The same may be true for many of you reading this now.

What I didn't realise at the time, and what no one (to my knowledge) has ever illustrated before, is that while these three verbs are difficult, the rest are, in comparison, easy. If the teacher had just added that one saving grace then I might have stayed tuned in a little longer. Instead, I was lost before I'd even begun. The task seemed too mammoth. The mountain too huge. Now, it is not enough for me to simply say 'The rest of it is easy' so I will explain exactly what I mean. I hope that, once you have heard the explanation, you will have had the first major insight into how I propose to help you learn the language, and give you a real sense of what this book is about and what it can do for you. Basically, it comes down to this. Avoir, Être, and Aller are the three most important verbs in the French language. Avoir means 'to have'. Être means 'to be'. Aller means 'to go'. (Apologies if you know all this, but we're going to start climbing our mountain at the bottom!). Think of a sentence in English. 'I'm going the shops.' 'I'm going to bed.' 'I'm tired.' 'I'm hungry.' Quite likely, the sentence you've just thought of contains one if not more of our three most important verbs. So, we learn these three because they are the most important. Secondly, because they are all irregular verbs, there are no short cuts. You have to learn them for what they are. They are individual and irregular and you just have to learn and practice them but, believe me, it's worth it and, at the end of the day, it's only three verbs. It's not the end of the world. Finally, these three verbs are the key to the past and future tenses. You cannot go backwards or forward in time in French without using these verbs. So, there are the three reasons why we learn Avoir, Être, and Aller: because they are the most important verbs; they are irregular so there are no shortcuts and you just have to learn them; and they are the key to the past and future tenses.

This is the bit that gets me, though. Why does no one tell you that, after learning those three verbs, the rest are easy. For the same amount of effort as it takes to learn just one of these verbs, if you conjugate just one regular 'ER' verb (that's a regular verb with an ER ending) you have access to more than ninety percent of all other

French verbs. If, for example, you learn how to conjugate Parler, which means 'to speak', then by learning the endings for that one ER verb, straight away you can use the same endings for ninety percent of all other French verbs, because the rule never, ever, ever, ever changes.

You conjugate Parler like this.

Je parle – I speak

Tu parles – You speak

Il/Elle parle – He/She speaks

Nous parlons – We speak

Vous parlez – You speak

Ils/Elles parlent – They speak.

As soon as you see another regular ER verb, you can use it, exactly as you did for Parler. If you see the verb Rester, which means 'to stay', you can use it straight away using the same ER endings.

Je reste – I stay

Tu restes – You stay

Il/Elle reste – He/She stays

Nous restons – We stay

Vous restez – You stay

Ils/Elles restent – They stay.

If you see the verb Manger, which means 'to eat', you can use it straight away.

Je mange – I eat

Tu manges – You eat

Il/Elle mange – He/She eats

Nous mangons – We eat (It's actually Nous mangeons but I'll explain all in the next chapter.)

Vous mangez – You eat

Ils/Elles mangent – They eat.

You open up a dictionary and come across a new verb, such as Parachuter, to parachute. Okay, you've never used that one before. You didn't know that the French word Parachuter meant 'to parachute' (although it's pretty obvious), but as soon as you recognise it as a regular ER verb (and given that more than ninety percent of all French verbs are regular ER verbs, nine times out of ten you're going to be right) then you can use it straight away.

So, let's try it for Parachuter.

Je parachute – I parachute

Tu parachutes – You parachute

Il/Elle parachute – He/She parachutes

Nous parachutons – We parachute

Vous parachutez – You parachute

Ils/Elles parachutent – They parachute.

Façile, non!

This rule for ER verbs is what I call The Golden Rule. I used to teach it to my Beginners group, and every week we would open up the dictionary at a random page and find a regular ER verb and conjugate it the same way. As I used to explain to them, in my own demanding style, by learning just one regular ER verb, they had access to more than ninety percent of all French verbs because the rule never, ever, ever, ever changes. If you've got a dictionary to hand, try it. How about Acheter, to buy; Lever, to lift; Laver, to wash, or Liberer, to liberate. All you have to do is remove the ER and then add the appropriate ending. Do it in that order. Take off the ER, then put in the correct ending, whether that's 'e' for Je, or 'es' for Tu, 'e' for Il and Elle, 'ons' for Nous, 'ez' for Vous, or 'ent' for Ils and Elles, just take off the ER and then add the right ending.

How does it feel to have immediate access to so many verbs? Do you feel empowered? Do you feel like climbing higher up the mountain? Me too. Let's read on.

Before we go, I'd just like to make a point that was raised by one of the students in my group. Why go to all the trouble of taking off the ER just to add some of it back. For example, for Je, add back the 'e', with Tu, we have to add back the 'e' and change the 'r' to an 's', and then for Il and Elle we add back the 'e' after we've taken it off. Why take something off and then add it back?

My reply is that The Golden Rule never ever changes. Learn it once, for one regular ER verb, and you can use it for ninety percent of all French verbs. It's easy enough. Don't be looking for shortcuts within The Golden Rule. You'll never climb the mountain like that. If you start by saying, for Je you just take off the R, for Tu you change the R to an S, for

Il and Elle you take off the R, etc, then you are going to end up doing that for every ER verb. You're making work for yourself. Every time you see a regular ER verb you're going to have to do that conjugation exercise all over again. If you eventually end up learning a thousand French verbs, you're going to have to do that exercise a thousand times. Is that a shortcut? I don't think so. Not when you can learn one rule, The Golden Rule. So don't think about dropping the 'r' for Je, etc. When you see a regular ER verb, just take off the ER and then apply the appropriate ending. For Je it is 'e'. For Tu it is 'es'. For Il and Elle it is 'e'. For Nous it is 'ons'. For Vous it is 'ez', and for Ils and Elles it is 'ent'. Take off the ER and then apply the relevant ending. That's The Golden Rule.

AVOIR, ÊTRE, and ALLER.

To have, to be, and to go. Avoir, Être, and Aller, the three most important verbs in the French language. They're all irregular, meaning that they don't follow a set pattern, so there are no shortcuts, and you're just going to have to learn them off by heart. But, then, you can't expect to climb your mountain and not break sweat! The good news is, it's only three verbs, and we're going to climb the mountain step by step.

Avoir – To have.

J'ai – I have

Tu as – You have

Il/Elle a – He/She has

Nous avons – We have

Vous avez – You have

Ils/Elles ont – They have.

Être – To be.

Je suis – I am

Tu es – You are

Il/Elle est – He/She is

Nous sommes – We are

Vous êtes – You are

Ils/Elles sont – They are.

Aller – To go.

Je vais – I go

Tu vas – You go

Il/Elle va – He/She goes

Nous allons – We go

Vous allez – You go

Ils/Elles vont – They go.

It should only take about a minute to recite all three. Try to do it at least once a week.

As stated, these are irregular verbs, however there are patterns everywhere you look in the French language. Look at the endings for the plural 'They'. For Avoir, it is Ont. For Être, it is Sont. For Aller, it is Vont. There are patterns everywhere. The more you learn, the fewer will be the gaps in your knowledge and you can start to utilise these patterns and shortcuts but, for now, let's learn them individually. Let's not look for shortcuts. We've a mountain to climb. If you're looking for shortcuts while you still at the bottom, you're likely to become disheartened. Better to embrace the challenge. You'll earn the right to use those shortcuts later on. That said, I'm not averse to a little 'aide-memoire' to help me along. When I'm struggling to remember the ending for 'They' for the verb Avoir, I think of owning something. To have is to own. Ils ont. They own. In the conjugation list for Être, you'll find Je suis and Nous sommes. The letter 's'. So in Être, for 'They', it's Ils sont. In Aller, you'll find Je vais, Tu vas, Il va, so the ending for 'They' is Ils vont, with a 'v'. Patterns everywhere you look, and there are lots of them in French. Hopefully, by the end of this book, you'll know most of them so that, even if you're unsure, you'll probably be able to make an educated guess, to employ a little gut-instinct and creativity. After all, it's your mountain to climb, and you're going to have to rely on your own skill and judgement to reach your goal. I can only help so much. I'll be your guide and your tipster, your mentor and supporter, but it's your mountain, your quest, and only you who can get you there. It's going to take effort, and probably only continued effort over a long period of time will get you to the summit, but many people still choose to take on the challenge, and many of those men and women ultimately succeed.

A word about the style and content of this book, of which more later. The more experienced among you will have spotted a couple of mistakes already in this book. For example, 'Nous mangeons' is the correct spelling. It employs an 'e' which isn't usually there (i.e. in 99.9% of the cases). However, I am making an important point here in explaining The Golden Rule. I'm more than happy to let the odd mistake slip through, and even to encourage you to make that mistake, in order to grasp the more important language lesson and to propel you further up the mountain. I'm assuming that English is your native language. I'm guessing you would call yourself fluent in your native tongue. Have you ever made a spelling mistake? Do you make them to this day? When you read letters or emails from colleagues, do they ever make mistakes in their spelling, grammar, or punctuation? I already know the answer. We probably all consider ourselves fluent and we all still make mistakes. Therefore, if we can make a few in English, we're certainly allowed to make them in French, especially while we're learning. So please, reader, if you spot a mistake, don't switch off and think the teacher (i.e. me in this instance) is an idiot, I'm probably making a bigger point, explaining a grander rule, for the greater good. That said (and I used to love it when my teachers did this in school!) I'm sure there'll be the odd 'deliberate' mistake in here too which I hadn't intended, in which case I can only ask your forgiveness. Hey, up on the mountain, we all occasionally slip. The trick is to pick yourself up and keep on walking. After all, we've a long way to go to get to the top.

THE GOLDEN RULE.

Michel Thomas is probably the world's foremost language expert. He has sold millions of books and CDs, and I'm a fan of his teaching methods. His gift for languages comes from a strange place. During the Second World War, he was working for the French Resistance when he was captured by the Vichy Government. Although French, the Vichy Government collaborated with Nazi Germany in order to be allowed to administer their own country. Michel Thomas was French. In all of his time in captivity, he never even saw a German soldier. His captors could have fed him cake and biscuits and told the Nazi's they were giving him a hard time. No one would ever have known. Instead, they tortured him. His own people, on behalf of a paymaster who never showed up.

According to Michel, in order to escape the pain of the torture, he would disappear into parts of his brain that he didn't know he had, in order to find some relief. When the war was over, Michel used that additional head-space in his expanded mind to learn a range of languages. His teaching methods really push your boundaries and offer a unique learning tool that serve to empower you. The CDs alone won't make you fluent but, used as part of a varied course of study, I believe they are one of the better tools for learning.

According to Michel, regular ER verbs make up more than ninety percent of all the verbs in the French language. Later in this book, I'm going to provide a list of many of the more common of these verbs. As you already know how to use them (using The Golden Rule), you immediately have access to them.

Let's look at a few.

Adapter – to adapt.

Admirer – to admire.

Adopter – to adopt.

Adorer – to adore.

Aider – to help.

Aimer – to love.

Amuser – to amuse.

Arranger – to arrange.

Arriver – to arrive.

Assister – to assist.

Anticiper – to anticipate.

And that's just the A's.

How would you say 'I adore that she's helping'?

The ending for Je (which means I) is E. The ending for Elle (which means She) is also E. Take of the ER and then add back the right ending.

J'ador<u>e</u> que Elle aid<u>e</u>.

You may have noticed, and I'm sure most of you already know, but Je, followed by a verb which starts with a vowel, becomes J'. The French language flows beautifully. It's one of the reasons that we often find it difficult to follow when learning the language. We can't see or hear the word breaks. The French love a bit of liaison in their language. They'll join their words together whenever possible. Je followed by a vowel becomes J'. In the example given above, the correct answer should have been 'J'ador_e_ qu'elle aid_e_' because the que becomes qu' when it is followed by a vowel. However, I didn't want to confuse you so I wrote it out in full. As you become more fluent, you can liaison all you like. For now, I'll stick to the elongated form if necessary for the purpose of clarity.

So, how would you say 'We adore that you are helping'?

The word for 'we' is Nous. The word for 'you' is Vous. (Yes, it can also be Tu. We'll come to that later. Let's use Vous for now, or use Tu if you prefer).

The first thing we do is take off the ER ending of Adorer (to adore) and Aider (to help).

Now add back the correct ending.

Nous ador_ons_ que vous aid_ez_.

By the way, I know that 'I adore that she is helping' or 'We adore that you are helping' are not the most common phrases that you are ever going to hear. Once again, I'm making a point. Once you have mastered The Golden Rule, you will be able to employ it in thousands of instances for thousands of verbs (there are about three thousand regular ER verbs in the French language, according to Michel

Thomas). Hopefully, you'll be able to express yourself a lot more naturally than 'I adore that she is helping'. More importantly, do you understand The Golden Rule?

CONSECUTIVE VERBS.

I've never really been strong on grammar. The terminology bores me, and I intend to keep it to a minimum in this book, however there is no getting away from it and we will have to address it at some point, although in no great detail. I believe that most of us learn a language through practice, and we pick up good grammar along the way. We probably all use adverbs and adjectives, etc, every time we open our mouths, without necessarily knowing the correct grammatical term for the words that we've just used. Instead, we just get on with it and say what we want to say, and usually we manage to make ourselves understood just fine. That's what we will do in this book, learn to communicate efficiently without focussing too much on grammar, except where it is an absolute necessity.

Usually, in a sentence, we will use a combination of subject, verb, and object. The subject is the person or thing that we are talking about. The verb is the thing that the person is doing. The object is the thing that the subject is doing the verb to. For example, the man ran to the car. In this sentence, the man is the subject, the running part is the verb, and the car is the object. That's as much as I'm going to say.

Now the verb is capable of being done in the present tense, i.e. it is happening as we speak, or in the past or the future. For example, I am running (present tense), I ran (past tense), I will run (future tense).

In French, when talking or writing in the present tense, you only have to conjugate the first verb. Any consecutive verbs are used in their entirety, making things really easy for you (and me!). If you want to say 'We love to help', it is Nous aim<u>ons</u> aider. If you want to say 'She loves to amuse her friends' you say Elle aim<u>e</u> amuser ses amis. If you want to say 'They love to parachute', it's Ils aim<u>ent</u> parachuter.

You conjugate the first verb. All subsequent verbs remain unaltered unless separated by 'that' or 'the' or some other word that breaks up the sentence. If it's a consecutive verb, you only need to conjugate the first one. This is true for two, three, or four verbs, or however many you can put into a sentence.

If you want to say 'He likes to help his pupils', it's Il aim<u>e</u> aider ses eleves.

In the present tense, for consecutive verbs, you only need to conjugate the first one. Subsequent verbs remain intact. This is true for all verbs, regular and irregular. The rules never change.

If you want to say 'I'm going to speak French', it's Je vais parler français.

If you want to say 'They adore speaking French', it's Ils adorent parler français.

You only conjugate the first verb in the present tense. For the remainder, you use the full verb.

If you break up the sentence and you have to start again, the rule still applies for consecutive verbs.

'I'm going to go to France and I'm going to speak French' would be Je vais aller en France et Je vais parler français.

The rule applies even when you use the same verb twice in a row, such as 'I'm going to go'. Je vais aller. You only conjugate the first verb. This is only true in the present tense. We'll do the past and future tenses later on, but this rule of consecutive verbs seems to me like a gift from the French language. You can now start to form much more elaborate sentences to help you get your point across.

Never forget to practice your three most important verbs, Avoir, Être, and Aller, and try to learn some new ER verbs, always remembering The Golden Rule. With just these simple constructs you can start to communicate more effectively.

For example, 'I'm going to be speaking French soon' is Je vais être parler français bientot.

You break it down. Je vais is 'I am going'. Être is 'to be'. Parler is 'to speak'.

Literally, what you are saying is 'I'm going to be to speak French soon'. However, we don't need to worry about literal translations. We are learning to speak French, and in the present tense, talking about what we are doing now, we only need to conjugate the first verb in the phrase or sentence. All the rest remain unchanged when they are consecutive verbs.

Here's another ER verb for you. Esperer, to hope.

J'esper<u>e</u> – I hope

Tu esper<u>es</u> – You hope

Il/Elle esper<u>e</u> – He/She hopes

Nous esper<u>ons</u> – We hope

Vous esper<u>ez</u> – You hope

Ils/Elles esper<u>ent</u> – They hope.

How do you say 'They hope to be speaking French soon'?

Think about it.

Start with 'They hope'.

Ils esperent.

To be is 'Être'. (It's one of your three main verbs, remember. Keep practicing those).

Speaking is 'Parler'.

French soon is 'français bientot'.

J'espere être parler français bientot.

Another way of saying this would be (I can feel the purists amongst you wanting to kill me!) 'J'espere que je vais être parler français bientot'. This translates as 'I hope that I'm going to be speaking French soon.' That is the more correct way of saying it. At the end of the day, we won't all climb the mountain at the same pace. Some will almost run up it. Others will walk. Some will take the smallest of steps.

J'espere être parler français bientot or J'espere que je vais être parler français bientot. It's your choice.

One other thing about the last sentence. Notice the use of 'que', meaning that. In English, we tend to omit the word when speaking or writing, even though it is implied and should, when using correct

English, be employed when implied. For example, if you say in English 'I hope I'm going to speak French soon', what you actually mean is 'I hope <u>that</u> I'm going to speak French soon'. In English, we usually omit it. In French, whenever it is implied, whenever it is meant to be there then you MUST use it. I'm not sure what the penalty is if you don't: blank stares probably, and possibly some mild contempt as the native speaker silently derides you for your inefficient use of the language. Anyway, I don't want to get you into trouble, and although I've already said that it's okay to make the odd mistake, I don't want to deliberately mislead you or get you into bad habits that may linger with you, so remember the rule. Whenever THAT is implied, when speaking in French, make sure you use it.

'J'espere <u>que</u> je vais être parler français bientot'.

Got it? D'accord. Bon travaille.

THE PAST TENSE.

What's with all this grammar, I hear you shout. 'You promised us that you wouldn't.' Well, I lied!

Remember the three most important verbs, Avoir, Être, and Aller? As stated earlier, as well as being the most important verbs for speaking in the present tense, they are also the key to the past and future tenses. Basically, you can't go backwards or forwards in the French language without using these verbs. So, we learn them for themselves (and remember to keep practising them), and they then allow us to talk about things that we were doing, and things that we are going to be doing, things that have happened and things that will happen, the past and the future.

For the past tense, we only need to use Avoir and Être. For the future tense, it will be Avoir and Aller. Nine times out of ten, when forming the past tense, you will use Avoir. Only for a very small number of verbs do you use Être and, luckily enough (thank you, French!), these are all verbs that are about movement, i.e. coming and going, living and dying, arriving and departing, going up and coming down, so they are related by theme. For all the rest you use Avoir. So, how do we conjugate Avoir? Do you remember? Have you been practising, i.e. spending just one minute at least once a week reciting all three of the most important verbs. You can say them out loud or say them to yourself. Leave a copy in the bathroom, put a copy in your purse or wallet and glance at it on the bus or in your lunch-hour or on the loo! This is how you conjugate Avoir, to have.

J'ai – I have

Tu as – You have

Il/Elle a – He/She has

Nous avons – We have

Vous avez – You have

Ils/Elles ont – They have.

Now here's the easy part.

To form the past tense in French, the construction is in three parts. The first two parts are listed above, i.e. 'J'ai' or 'Tu as', etc. The third and final part is what is known as the past participle. Every French verb has a past participle. They are all unique, but they all follow a rule. For regular ER verbs, more than ninety percent of all French verbs, the rule is a simple one. You take off the R and you put an accent over the 'e'. This is true for all regular ER verbs.

Note, if you want to take off the ER and add back an é, you can do. Whatever works best for you, works for me. Either way, the past participle for every regular ER verb looks like this.

For parler, it is parlé.

For manger, it is mangé.

For parachuter, it is parachuté.

For acheter, it is acheté. (Acheter means 'to buy'.)

For adapter, it is adapté.

For admirer, it is admiré.

For adopter, it is adopté.

For adorer, it is adoré.

For aider, it is aidé.

For aimer, it is aimé.

For amuser, it is amusé.

For arranger, it is arrangé.

For assister, it is assisté.

For anticiper, it is anticipé.

So, to say 'he spoke', you use the first two parts from Avoir and the past participle of parler. What you are really saying is 'he has spoken', Il a parlé.

She has eaten, Elle a mangé.

They parachuted, Ils ont parachuté.

He bought, Il a acheté.

We adapted, Nous avons adapté.

You admired, Tu as admiré, or Vous avez admiré. The past participle never changes.

He adopted, Il a adopté.

I adored, J'ai adoré.

They helped, Ils ont aidé.

We loved, Nous avons aimé.

She amused, Elle a amusé.

You arranged, Tu as arrangé, or Vous avez arrangé.

He assisted, Il a assisté.

They anticipated, Ils ont anticipé.

We'll discuss accents in greater detail later on. For now, all you need to know is that the accent over the E, in this instance, is called an Accent Aigu. An accent is just an aid to pronunciation. When reading the word, you should ignore it. (Again I can hear the purists cry 'foul'. I'll explain more later but, while trying to learn a new word, when reading it, just ignore the accent and concentrate on the word itself. Don't be confused by the accent). For pronunciation purposes, an accent aigu, which only ever occurs over the letter E, gives the letter an 'ay' sound, like in day, way, or say. For the regular ER verb conjugation of the past participle, for example parlé, the word sounds exactly the same as when you say the full verb Parler. This is true for all regular ER verbs. The past participle (always just remove the ER and add an é on the end) sounds exactly the same as the full verb. This is true for Mangé, sounds exactly the same as Manger, Parachuté sounds exactly the same as Parachuter, Adapté sounds exactly the same as Adapter, and so on and so forth, for every regular ER verb.

Now you know how to form the past tense of more than ninety percent of all French verbs, using just Avoir and the past participle rule, which is to take off the ER and put é on the end.

You may have noticed that there were a couple of words missing from the list above, words that we've been using up to now. They are Rester, Aller, and Arriver. Okay, Aller, as an irregular verb, shouldn't really be here, but as it shares the same function for forming the past participle, I'm going to include it. Like I said earlier, there are patterns everywhere you look in the French language.

Rester, Aller, and Arriver all form the past participle in exactly the same way as every other regular ER verb. The rule never ever changes. Do you remember it? (I hope so. It was only six lines ago!) Take off the ER and add back é. As I said before, you are welcome to think of it as taking off the R and putting an accent over the E, whichever works best for you. I only allow this for forming the past participle. When conjugating a regular ER verb in the present tense, use The Golden Rule. Don't waver from the path. You'll only make more work for yourself.

So, let's form the past participle of Rester, Aller, and Arriver. Take off the ER and add back an é.

Rester is resté.

Aller is allé.

Arriver is arrivé.

So why didn't I include these earlier? Why did I leave them out? Do you know?

I'm sure many of you know the answer. It's because these are verbs of movement, coming and going, which also includes staying. As such, they are formed using Être. The first two parts of the three part construct come from Être. The third part is just to employ the past participle. How do we conjugate Être?

Je suis – I am

Tu es – You are

Il/Elle est – He/She is

Nous sommes – We are

Vous êtes – You are

Ils/Elles sont – They are.

Now say 'I stayed'.

Je suis resté.

Now say 'He went'.

Il est allé.

Now say 'They arrived'.

Ils sont arrivé.

C'est façile, non? Bon travaille, mes eleves. Bon travaille.

Now I'm sure many of you will be wondering how to form the past participle for irregular verbs and for those verbs that aren't regular ER verbs, such as RE verbs like Prendre (to take) or IR verbs such as Partir (to leave) or OIR verbs such as Voir (to see), well, we'll get to that later on. For now, give yourself a pat on the back for learning the past tense for ninety percent of all the verbs in the French language. That's not bad for a short chapter's reading!

THE FUTURE TENSE.

As we have seen, we can't go backwards in French without using Avoir and Être. We can't use the past tense, to talk about things that have already happened, without using two of our three most important verbs. Neither can we go forward in time, to talk about things that we are going to do in the future without using another two of our three main verbs, this time, Avoir and Aller. Once again, this illustrates the importance of learning those three irregular verbs off by heart, by practicing as often as you can, at least once a week. It only takes a minute to recite all three. I'm going to say them again for the benefit of all, myself included.

Avoir – To have.

J'ai – I have

Tu as – You have

Il/Elle a – He/She has

Nous avons – We have

Vous avez – You have

Ils/Elles ont – They have.

Être – To be.

Je suis – I am

Tu es – You are

Il/Elle est – He/She is

Nous sommes – We are

Vous êtes – You are

Ils/Elles sont – They are.

Aller – To go

Je vais – I go

Tu vas – You go

Il/Elle va – He/She goes

Nous allons – We go

Vous allez – You go

Ils/Elles vont – They go.

To form the future tense and talk about things that we are going to do, there are two ways to go about it. You can choose either or use both. The good news is, they're both easy!

I'll start with the more difficult of the two. Essentially, we will be using Avoir and Aller. We don't need to bother with Être.

Using Avoir to form the future tense of a regular ER verb.

The French literally say 'I to speak have'. Je parler ai. 'He to speak has.' Il parler a. 'You to speak have.' Vous parler ez. 'We to speak have.' Nous parler ons. What they mean is, I have to speak, he has to speak, you have to speak, we have to speak. It's just the way the French set their grammar out.

Over the course of time, when speaking, the French tended to bunch the words together so that 'I have to speak' or 'I to speak have' became Je parlerai. They dragged the ending into the word. So, for regular ER verbs, you use the full word followed by the appropriate ending. For Je it is 'ai', for Tu it is 'as', for Il and Elle it is 'a', for Nous it is 'ons', for Vous it is 'ez', and for Ils and Elles it is 'ent'. This is true for all regular ER verbs.

Je mangerai – I will eat.

Tu resteras – You will stay.

Il adaptera – He will adapt.

Elle admirera – She will admire.

Nous adopterons – We will adopt.

Vous parachuterez – You will parachute.

Elle achetera – She will buy.

Ils adorerent – They will adore.

Elles aimerent – They will love.

J'espererai – I will hope.

Tu aideras – You will help.

Il amusera – He will amuse.

Elle arrangera – She will arrange.

Nous laverons – We will wash.

Vous arriverez – You will arrive.

Nous travaillerons – We will work.

Ils assisterent – They will assist.

Elles anticiperent – They will anticipate.

Je leverai – I will lift.

Tu libereras – You will liberate.

For regular ER verbs, more than ninety percent of all French verbs, you use the full verb followed by the correct Avoir ending for the appropriate subject. Je is 'ai', etc.

This is also true for the IR verbs, (all except Venir – to come) so now, you're probably up to ninety five percent of all French verbs where you can use this rule. Try it for Sortir – to go out, and Partir – to leave.

Je sortirai – I will go out.

Tu sortiras – you will go out.

Il sortira – He will go out.

Elle sortira – She will go out.

Nous sortirons – We will go out.

Vous sortirez – You will go out.

Ils sortirent – They will go out.

Elles sortirent – They will go out.

Je partirai – I will leave.

Tu partiras – You will leave.

Il partira – He will leave.

Elle partira – She will leave.

Nous partirons – We will leave.

Vous partirez – You will leave.

Ils partirent – They will leave.

Elles partirent – They will leave.

For RE endings, you simply drop the E and add the appropriate Avoir ending. For example, for Prendre – to take, you drop the E and add the ending.

Je prendrai – I will take.

Tu prendras – You will take.

Il prendra – He will take.

Elle prendra – She will take.

Nous prendrons – We will take.

Vous prendrez – you will take.

Ils prennent – They will take.

Elle prennent. They will take.

Okay, the last one changed slightly. They dropped the D. No matter. If we know it, great. If we make a mistake, I'm sure we'll be forgiven. After all, we're trying our best to speak a foreign language. We'll usually get some marks for effort. At least we're trying.

Tip – listen out for the R sound. Every French future tense construction with Avoir employs this sound towards the end of the word, giving you a good sound clue that we are dealing with the future tense (apart, I've just realised, from prennent, which only uses it at the beginning. Oh well, I guess there is an exception to every rule, and in French, there are lots and lots of exceptions!)

Another way to form the future tense is even easier. Just use Aller, to go, followed by the full verb of whatever it is that you're going to do. For example:

Je vais rester – I'm going to stay.

Tu vas partir – You are going to leave.

Il va sortir – He is going to go out.

Elle va parachuter – She is going to parachute.

Nous allons manger – We are going to eat.

Vous allez parler – You are going to speak.

Ils vont assister – They are going to assist.

Elles vont adapter – They are going to adapt.

Some of you may have been thrown a little as you went down the list when you got to Nous and Vous. You were comfortable with Vais, Vas, and Va, and then we suddenly got to Allons and Allez. Don't be thrown by it. If you've learned Aller, as one of your three main verbs, then you should know it by heart.

Again, that's another reason why we learn our three most important verbs, and why we should practice them at least once a week. If you can't find a minute in your week for that, then I honestly don't think that you're ever going to climb the mountain.

WHY IS GRAMMAR SO IMPORTANT ?

I managed to get through most of my life without understanding grammar. I had no idea what an adverb was, or an adjective. Yes, I knew what a verb was, and a noun, but I saw no need to understand the terminology or the rules. It just wasn't necessary. It wasn't important. I managed perfectly well without it. So what is grammar, exactly? And why is it important.

One member of my Beginners group once told me a story. He used to work with a man who had come to Britain from overseas. The man used to ask him, on an almost daily basis, 'Which time is it?' Now, this used to make my student smile. He found the incorrect use of English quite funny, but he still understood the question. The foreign man wanted to know the time. Instead of 'What time is it?', he would ask 'Which time is it?'. But, guess what, he'd still managed to make himself understood, in a way, and my student used to tell the man the time. The foreigner asked a question and got the answer he wanted, even if he hadn't asked it quite correctly. Don't be afraid to make mistakes. Even if you're nearly right, or only part right, you're communicating. I'm sure at some point, this man is going to correct himself. At some point along his journey, when the penny drops, or when he's been corrected enough times, he's going to start asking 'What time is it?' For now, 'Which time is it?' still serves its purpose.

The actor Christopher Waltz, star of several Tarantino movies, was recently talking about the grammar of acting. He said that he had a tutor who taught him an important lesson. The scenario ran like this. A man walks up to a hotdog seller and says 'Hot me a give dog'. Now, the hotdog seller, being in the business, can pretty much guess what his customer wants, but he has to configure the sentence in such a way that it makes sense, and he probably has to go back to the customer just to be sure. 'So, you want a hot dog?' And the customer says yes and the transaction takes place. But, if the customer had just said 'Give me a hot dog', with all the words in the right place in the first instance, no further communication would have been necessary. The customer asks, the hot dog vendor gives, and it's deal done. That's what good grammar is. All the words in the right order. What it allows for is effective and direct communication. There is no need for further explanation. 'Is that what you want, buddy? A hot dog?' Straight away, if the customer makes his request using the correct grammar then everything is understood.

That's what you should aspire to, all the words in the right order but, in the first instance, 'Which time is it?' still gets the job done. Don't be afraid to make mistakes.

THE IMPERFECT TENSE.

The imperfect tense is kind of an informal version of the past tense. It is all about events that happened in the past, but it is used for things that didn't just happen, but were happening, or used to happen. For example, 'I read a book' is the past tense. That action is complete. It's perfect. 'I was reading a book' is the imperfect tense. I'm guessing there's more to that story (no pun intended). 'I was reading a book when there was a knock on the door', that sort of thing. Think of it as an informal version of the past tense. The good news is, it is fairly easy to use, and together with our present, past, and future tenses, it's one of the important ones that you need to learn. It is used very often in French. Don't worry, we're only go to do one more tense after this one, the conditional, which we will get to in a little while.

The stem of the word, and the letter 'I' are the clues that I remember for the imperfect tense. When we use The Golden Rule, what we do is take off the ER before adding back the appropriate ending for the person we're talking about. The part of the word that is left after removing the ER is known as the stem. So, for Parler, the stem is 'Parl'. For Manger, it is 'Mang', and so on. Forming the imperfect is easy for regular ER verbs. All you have to do is take off the ER to leave the stem and then add the following endings.

For Je, it is AIS.

For Tu, it is AIS.

For Il and Elle it is AIT.

For Nous it is IONS.

For Vous it is IEZ.

For Ils and Elles it is AIENT.

So, how would you say 'I was speaking'?

Je parl<u>ais</u>.

How would you say 'You were eating'?

Tu mang<u>ais</u>.

How would you say 'He was staying'?

Il rest<u>ait</u>.

How would you say 'She was parachuting'?

Elle parachut<u>ait</u>.

How would you say 'We were buying'?

Nous achet<u>ions</u>.

How would you say 'You were working'?

Vous travaill<u>iez</u>.

How would you say 'They were helping (masculine)'?

Ils aid<u>aient</u>.

How would you say 'They were arranging (feminine)'?

Elles arrang<u>aient</u>.

C'est façile.

Notice how each of these endings contains the letter 'I'. That's how I remember it. I for imperfect.

Notice also that the imperfect endings for Je and Tu end with an S, and the endings for Il and Elle end with a T. You'll come across a similar thing later on when we do endings for irregular verbs. Like I've said before, there are patterns everywhere you look in French. Anyway, now you know the imperfect tense.

C'est très façile. C'est simple. And remember the imperfect endings. You're going to use them again to form the conditional tense.

THE CONDITIONAL TENSE.

This is the last of the tenses that we are going to cover in this book. There are others, such as the subjunctive, but I think we're getting out of our depth. I'm trying to spur you on, not kill your spirit. This book won't be the only one you need to read in order to learn French. You're going to learn like a kid does, and expose yourself to as many opportunities, and place yourselves in as many French-speaking environments as possible, in order to master the language or improve your language skills. Basically, between the present tense, that past and future tenses, the imperfect and the conditional, you've probably covered about eighty percent of the tenses in the French language. I think that's enough for you right now.

So what is the conditional tense? Essentially, it's used where you want to qualify a statement. We are talking about things where we might like to include the words 'would', 'could', or 'should'. You might want to say 'I could speak now' or 'I should eat now' or 'I would stay now'. So how do we do it? Again, c'est façile.

To form the conditional tense for a regular ER verb, more than ninety percent of all verbs, all you do is take the full verb and add the imperfect tense endings. So for Parler, or whichever verb you want to use, you take the whole word and add on the appropriate ending for whoever you're talking about.

I would speak is 'Je parler<u>ais</u>'.

You should eat is 'Tu manger<u>ais</u>'.

He could stay is 'Il rester<u>ait</u>'.

We should buy is 'Nous acheter<u>ions</u>'.

She could adapt is 'Elle adapter<u>ait</u>'.

We could adopt is 'Nous adopter<u>ions</u>'.

You would love is 'Vous aimer<u>iez</u>'.

They could arrive (masculine) is 'Ils arriver<u>aient</u>'.

They should assist (feminine) is Elles assister<u>aient</u>'.

Instead of using just the stem of the word, as you do for the imperfect tense, you use the full verb followed by the imperfect endings. The future tense also uses the full verb, followed by the regular Avoir endings, so the conditional tense and the future tense are very similar. Patterns everywhere.

Irregular verbs are different, and we'll deal with these later. They're not hard, but there are no shortcuts, unfortunately, and you just have to learn them for what they are. The good news is that for verbs ending in IR, like Finir – to finish, the conditional tense also uses the full verb. So 'I should finish' is Je finirais. You should finish is Tu finirais. He should finish is Il finirait. She should finish is Elle finirait. We should finish is Nous finirions. You should finish is Vous finiriez. They should finish (masculine) is Ils finiraient. They should finish (feminine) is Elles finiraient.

Similarly, French verbs ending in RE are also easy to form in the conditional tense. All you do is drop the E at the end and then add the imperfect tense endings. For the verb Prendre – to take, it goes like this.

I would take is 'Je prendrais'. You would take is 'Tu prendrais'. He would take is Il prendrait. She would take is Elle prendrait. We would take is Nous prendrions. You would take is Vous prendriez. They would take (masculine) is Ils prendraient. They would take (feminine) is Elles prendraient.

That's your five main tenses covered. Now you're speaking French!

HOW TO FORM THE NEGATIVE IN FRENCH.

Every action has an equal and opposite reaction. That's a law of the universe. Therefore, if we're spending time learning how TO do something, we should also take a look at how NOT TO do something.

It may at first seem complicated. It's not. It's easy. The trick is not to get confused. It can seem a bit much, because you have to drop in something before and after the verb, making a two word statement into a four word statement, but it really isn't difficult at all.

Here's how we say 'I speak'. Je parle.

Here's how we say 'I don't speak'. Je ne parle pas.

We put a 'ne' in front of the verb and 'pas' after it. Simple, non!

How do we say 'He eats'? Il mange.

How do we say 'He doesn't eat'? Il ne mange pas. C'est très façile.

The word 'ne' doesn't actually mean anything at all. It is there purely to give an indication to the listener that we are about to use a negation. That we <u>aren't</u> going to do something. Think 'ne' for negative. 'Pas' means 'not'. There are other negative endings as well, such as the word RIEN for nothing, JAMAIS for never, and PLUS for no longer. They are all formed exactly the same way. Subject, followed by 'ne', followed by verb, followed by whichever negative word you're using: not, nothing, never, or no longer.

So, let's try a few out.

He never speaks is 'Il ne parle jamais'.

You never help is 'Tu ne aides jamais' (although you would actually use 'n'aides' for liaison purposes).

We have nothing is 'Nous n'avons rien'.

They no longer parachute is 'Ils ne parachutent plus'.

How do you say 'I want' ? It is Je veux.

How would you say 'I don't want'? It is Je ne veux pas. (We'll do Vouloir, which means 'to want', later on.)

Now the thing about language, and people, is that they love a shortcut. Although all of the above is correct, you will often hear French people dispense with the 'ne' part. They'll just say 'Il parle jamais', or whichever example you prefer. Their thinking is, I'm saying 'never', (i.e. jamais), so why should I bother giving you the signal that I'm going to use a negation, and they leave it out. However, correct French insists that you use it, especially in the written word form, although people do often leave it out when speaking.

When I was at university, I first heard people dropping the 'ne' part. I was a mature student at the time. I'd already graduated from two universities, however this urge to learn French had never gone away and I thought, if I don't start now, it's probably never going to happen. In reality though, I was in the wrong place at the wrong time and I left after a year, frustrated with the course and with myself.

Some of the younger guys would say stuff like 'Je sais pas'. This is the abbreviated form of 'Je ne sais pas', which means 'I don't know'. These people had obviously spent some time in France, at summer school or whatever, and because they were young and cool, they'd take the shortcut. Please don't be tempted to take the shortcut. It's better to be correct than to be cool, especially when you're learning.

In all, I found my year at university frustrating for several reasons. Obviously, I was much older than the other students, so that wasn't great, however at least it meant I was free to concentrate on my studies, not having to go overboard on the social side of things. I'd already done my student-partying years earlier. More than anything, I just wasn't happy with the amount of French I was being taught. All the lessons were in English. Plus, in order to get on to the course, I'd had to choose a second subject, and took English Language, so I was getting English on top of English when I wanted to be learning French! In the whole academic year, my actual course requirement to speak French was a total of thirty minutes, i.e. three ten minutes of French conversation with one of the tutors. I thought this was tragic. Instead, I'd go into the labs and watch French tv and try and make the most of the resources. For now, I'd sum it up like this.

As I've said, I had previously graduated from two universities, gaining a HND and a Master's degree. If you are eighteen, nineteen, or twenty, I would say 'go to university' (although I was actually twenty six when I attended my first university, so please don't let me put you off!). You'll find a good balance between work and play, make some great friends along the way, and come out with a qualification that will put you on equal footing with anyone chasing the same career prospects as yourself. I would also recommend that you try to draw the minimum amount of loans possible to pay for your studies. You're going to be a long time paying them off, because a university degree doesn't usually come cheap.

I was forty two when I decided to go back to university to learn French. I left a good job, and quickly forgot what it was like to have money in my pocket. I was struggling to pay my bills, unable to pay my rent, sitting in a language lab watching episodes of French soap operas and hardly understanding a word. No wonder I was depressed. So I left after a year and tried to get my life back on track. Now, although I'm learning French at a much slower pace than I'd like, at least I have my life back in perspective. As my friend Marcus once remarked, 'Plan your life like a bank robbery. Make sure you've got several escape routes!' I'd put all of my eggs in one basket in order to learn French, but there are so many other ways in which to go about it. Find the one that suits you best. Though I'm not exactly racing for the summit, I still hope that one day I'll get there. And you can too.

If I was forty two again and wanted to learn French, I would not go to university. I'd take a sabbatical and use the resources available on the internet and at the local library, or, even better, head off to France for a few months, as I once did. If I had the money, I'd book an immersion course for a couple of weeks or a month if possible. They're not cheap, but I'd rather spend five grand living like a king and learning more in a month than spending an unproductive first year at uni. These immersion courses are popular with business people who are relocating overseas. They do a good job and they work you really hard. They have you listening to French and speaking the language all day every day for the duration of your stay. I reckon you'd be about half way up the mountain by the end of it. If you stayed in the country afterwards, for work or whatever, I think you'd be pretty close to the summit after a year. That's the way I'd go. If I couldn't go abroad, I'd spend a couple of hours a week with a personal tutor if I could afford it. Top the lessons up with your own studies and you'll be climbing all the time. Not as quick as immersion but moving up all the same. Get yourself a range of CDs, some kids' story books, some grammar exercise tutorials, and find a French class nearby. As long as you're moving, as long as you're practicing, you're climbing up the mountain.

FAIRE. THE FOURTH MOST IMPORTANT VERB.

As you know, I'm a big believer in the three most important verbs and The Golden Rule. Now that we've come so far, I think it's time to broaden our horizons slightly, to maybe set off from Base Camp and venture a little higher. I came to realise, when teaching my Beginners group, that we were not giving due respect and attention to the fourth most important verb, Faire, which means 'to do' or 'to make'.

After we'd done the three most important verbs, and The Golden Rule, we'd then do Faire. We'd do it twice. Once as 'to do' and once as 'to make'. Let's try it. We'll do it first as 'To Do'.

Je fais – I do

Tu fais – You do

Il fait – He does

Elle fait – She does

Nous faisons – We do

Vous faites – You do

Ils font – They do

Elles font – They do.

Notice the endings for the Je and Tu conjugation. It's the letter 'S'. Notice the endings for the Il and Elle conjugations. It's the letter 'T'. We've seen that already with the imperfect tense endings. You're going to see a lot more of it too when we look at the other verb endings, i.e. for RE, IR, and OIR verbs. It's one of the most regular sightings in French for all the verbs which aren't regular ER verbs, i.e. the other ten percent. You'll start to notice it, and soon you'll start to expect it. You can make an educated guess that it should be there, and nine times out of ten you will be right. Where does that put us now? Ninety nine percent? I'm only kidding. But it's true that there are patterns everywhere in French.

Let's do Faire again. This time as 'To Make'.

Je fais – I make

Tu fais – You make

Il fait – He makes

Elle fait – She makes

Nous faisons – We make

Vous faites – You make

Ils font – They make

Elles font – They make.

Notice the ending for 'They'. It is Ils font. Recognise that? Along with the other three most important verbs, it shares a similar ending. Now we have 'ont', 'sont', 'vont', and 'font'. This doesn't happen anywhere else in the French language, but the four most important verbs share a similar ending for 'They'. 'Ont', 'sont', 'vont', and 'font'. There are patterns everywhere in French.

By the way, notice how the Vous form of Faire doesn't end in 'ez'. There are only three examples in the entire French language where the Vous form of the verb does not end in 'ez'. These are Vous êtes (with Être), Vous faites (with Faire) and Vous dites (with Dire, which mean 'To Say). Otherwise, in every other instance, the ending of ANY verb in the Vous form will be EZ. Got it? Bon.

IN SPEAKING, FOLLOW THE SOUND OF 'I'.

We're learning a lot of French here. Some tips, lots of tenses. We're learning the rules, hopefully having a little fun, and preparing ourselves to climb up the mountain. The thing is though, theory is all well and good, but what about the practice? What happens when you come to actually speak to a French person, or watch a bit of French telly, or listen to French radio, or join a French conversation group. How are you going to interact? How are we going to understand the spoken word?

Remember our regular ER verbs? They make up ninety percent of ALL French verbs. Well here's how to pronounce them. All three thousand of them because the rules for regular ER verbs never, ever, ever, ever change.

How do you say 'I speak'?

It is Je parle. You pronounce it Je (like zjuh) parle (parl). You pronounce the last consonant (L) of parle, and the final 'e' is silent.

Every other conjugation, apart from the 'nous' and 'vous' form, has the same pronunciation.

Je parle, Tu parle, Il parles, and Elle parle all sound exactly the same. Parle, parles, parle, parle all sound the same.

For the Ils and Elles versions, they sound almost exactly the same. The only difference is that they linger slightly longer on the final 'L' sound. They sound like Ils parLL, although its spelt Ils parlent. The 'ent' ending is silent for regular ER verbs. So it's Ils and Elles parLL, and Je, Tu, Il, and Elle parL in pronunciation. It only changes for the Nous and the Vous form. Nous parlons and Vous parlez.

Now you're speaking French, and if you want to climb up the mountain, you have to find as many opportunities as possible to do so. Even talking to yourself works (or maybe that's just me!). If you can't find a French speaker to converse with, get yourself a long-wave radio and listen to some French programmes, or tune in to some French tv if you have satellite, or check out the millions of videos available in French on Youtube. Find ways in which to practice speaking or listening to French. If you can't find a French speaker, talk to yourself. Tell yourself about your day, your week, or what you're planning to do tomorrow. Got no plans, make something up.

Je vais parachuter aujourd'hui. Je vais acheter une voiture demain. J'ai un rendez-vous avec le docteur apres-midi. Je suis malade. Je vais regarder la television ce soir. J'ai un rendez-vous avec une grande vedette, Brigitte Bardot! Je vais parler français tout la journée. C'est façile, non? Je parlerai français bientot.

ACCENTS ARE ONLY AN AID TO PRONUNCIATION.

When you look at any of the words in the French vocabulary or verb lists within this book, or any time you see a French word that has an accent in it, I want you to try and read the word first without looking at the accent. Ignore the accent. It makes it easier to recognize the word. The accent is only there as an aid to pronunciation. It tells you how you should pronounce the word. Here are the main types of accent that you will come across.

The accent aigu is the most common. It is the one that slopes up towards the right, as in é. It only ever appears over the letter 'e' and tells you that the é should be pronounced 'ay', as in day, way, or say.

Another common accent is the grave accent. This is the mirror image of the accent aigu, with the line sloping upwards but backwards toward the previous letter. This tells you that the letter should have a short, sharp sound, i.e. it is not to be prolonged in any way. The grave accent can appear over any vowel, such as over the letter 'e' in 'très' meaning 'very', or as in 'où' meaning 'where'. It doesn't really make much difference in spoken French, so you don't have to worry about it too much, but you must remember to use it in writing. If you write 'ou' without the accent, instead of meaning 'where' it means 'or', so it's important that you include it.

The circumflex accent (circonflexe in French) is the little rooftop accent. It usually symbolizes a vanished letter 'S' after the vowel, as in the words 'hôpital' for hospital, or 'hôtesse' for hostess. It doesn't alter the pronunciation of the French word, however, and this accent may one day disappear from use as time goes on. It will probably become redundant as it isn't doing enough to earn its place in the language.

The cedilla accent is the little tail that appears under the letter 'c' in certain words, such as français. It indicates that the letter should be pronounced with a soft 's' sound rather than a hard 'c' sound. Without the cedilla, français would probably be pronounced franKais. Now we pronounce it franSais. You won't find it used to often in French but, again, when you do see it, remember it's just an aid to pronunciation.

You may also have come across the diaeresis accent, known in French as the trema. This is the name for the two little dots that appear in words such as 'coïncidence', 'Noël', and Moët. The accent only ever appears on the second of two consecutive vowels, and it tells you to pronounce the vowels separately. So for Noel, you pronounce it No-el. There's no flow through the word. When you see the trema, remember to say the two vowels as two separate syllables.

You'll see lots of accents in written French. They are only an aid to pronunciation, and if the word looks foreign to you, try reading it without the accent. You may just get a pleasant surprise.

WAYS IN WHICH TO LEARN.

What is the best way to learn French? Learn as if you're learning English all over again. I have a friend, Colin, who is learning Mandarin. Don't ask me why. Now, we think that we've got a mountain to climb. His is higher. I asked him recently, on a percentage level, what degree of fluency did he think he had attained. He said eighty percent. He's four-fifths of the way up his mountain. I asked him the secret. What is the best way to learn a language, in his opinion? I already knew the answer, in some way. Is it practice, practice, practice, I asked? Yes, he said. Expose yourself to the language in every way possible, was his advice. Listen to the radio, watch tv in that language, get some exercise books, find a native speaker to converse with. In other words, surround yourself, immerse yourself. Whenever you're working with and in that language, you're learning. Even if it's just for ten minutes a day, reading or doing your grammar exercises, or sitting on the loo reciting your three main verbs, you're putting one foot in front of the other and moving up the mountain. Sometimes, you may still be circling around the base. It doesn't matter. You're building solid foundations and the knowledge will come in handy some day.

Colin's advice was to learn your chosen foreign language, in our case French, the same way as if you were learning English all over again. Cast your mind back. Honestly, take a minute to reflect. You were a child. You had toys. These probably had some educational aspect. You'd learn the colours, numbers, eventually the alphabet (wow, wasn't that exciting! I remember my cousin teaching it to me, and boy did I feel liberated, knowledgeable, and powerful). With my Beginners group, we used to do the Alphabet every week. In all the ways that I had sought to learn French, at school, college, and university, I don't ever remember anyone teaching me the Alphabet. We might have brushed over it, but we never used to practice it. I felt like a fraud. There I was, at university, trying to learn French and yet I didn't even know the French Alphabet. So, with my Beginners group, we would do it every week. It's the most solid of building blocks. Everything stems from it. I urge you to learn it.

As my Beginners group used to meet informally, and as I was just a volunteer tutor, I didn't want to task them with anything as onerous as homework. One, they probably wouldn't do it and would feel guilty about it. Two, it just wouldn't be fun. Yet I had to give them something to do, so I asked each of them to bring a new word for the following week. That was it. Just learn one new word. I asked that it be a noun, preferably the name of an everyday object. That was easy enough. If they had forgotten, they could just open up their dictionaries and pick something out at random. It was easy. Each week I would ask them 'Avez-vous un nouveau mot?' Yes, they would say. 'Qu'est ce que c'est?' I would ask.

They would say their new word.

'Pouvez-vous épeller le mot pour nous?' I would ask. And they would spell out the word.

The rest of the group would have to write down the letters as they were read out. This reinforced our Alphabet learning. Afterwards, we'd check to see that we had all written it down correctly. There were usually about six people in my group. Each week, that's six new words. Slowly, as well as reinforcing our Alphabet learning, we were improving our vocabulary. After ten weeks, that's sixty new words. That's why I asked for everyday objects. It's no use learning the word for 'ostrich feather'. How often are you going to use it? Maybe one day, when you're four-fifths of the way up the mountain, you might need to learn that. For now, let's stick with table, lamp, and desk. Everyday objects. Carpet, curtains, wall, book, coat. That sort of thing. So, learn like you were learning English all over again. Challenge yourself, immerse yourself, and don't be afraid to make mistakes.

The Alphabet is covered on many of the French language CDs. You can also go on Youtube, just type in the words 'French Alphabet' in the search space and you'll find a video of someone doing the French Alphabet pronunciations. It will be directed at kids, or at people trying to learn like yourselves. Copy and practice, and don't try to climb the mountain until you know how to say it.

IRREGULAR VERBS ARE THE FINAL FRONTIER.

The three most important verbs in French are all irregular. So is the fourth, Faire. I guess it's time we addressed the fact that not everything in our garden is rosy, and in order to learn the French language, we're going to have to do some hard work.

You all now know how to conjugate Avoir, Être, Aller, and Faire in the present tense. Let's look at those verbs in the past and future tenses.

For the past tense, we will need to know the past participle. For Avoir, it is 'eu'. For Être it is 'été', and for Aller it is allé. For Faire it is 'fait'.

I had is 'J'ai eu'.

I have been is 'J'ai été.

I went is 'Je suis allé'. (The past tense is formed with Être in this instance as it's a verb of movement).

I did or I made is 'J'ai fait', (Tu as fait, Il/Elle a fait, Nous avons fait, Vous avez fait, Ils/Elles ont fait).

There's an easier way to say 'I had' or 'I was'. Use the imperfect form. J'avais is 'I had'. J'etait is 'I was'.

Because these verbs are all irregular, they also have irregular stems with which to form the future tense. Luckily enough, these stems can then be used to form the conditional tense of the words, so they're well worth learning. That's two tenses for the price of one. Again, there are no shortcuts. You just have to learn them.

The future stem of Avoir is AUR.

The future stem of Être is SER.

The future stem of Aller is IR.

The future stem of Faire is FER.

To form the future tense, we then add the endings from the present tense of Avoir, just as we would to form the future tense for regular ER verbs.

So, for Avoir, we conjugate the verb in the future tense like this.

Je aurai – I will have (although you shorten it to J'aurai because of the vowel liaison)

Tu auras – You will have

Il aura – He will have

Elle aura – She will have

Nous aurons – We will have

Vous aurez – You will have

Ils auront – They will have (instead of the 'ent' ending, for these irregular verbs it changes to 'ont')

Elles auront – They will have.

For Être, it goes like this.

Je serai – I will be

Tu seras – You will be

Il sera – He will be

Elle sera – She will be

Nous serons – We will be

Vous serez – You will be

Ils seront – They will be

Elles seront – They will be.

For Aller, it goes like this.

Je irai – I will go (although you shorten it to J'irai because of vowel liaison)

Tu iras – you will go

Il ira – He will go

Elle ira – She will go

Nous irons – we will go

Vous irez – You will go

Ils iront – They will go

Elles iront – They will go.

For Faire, it goes like this.

Je ferai – I will do/make

Tu feras – You will do/make

Il fera – He will do/make

Elle fera – She will do/make

Nous ferons – We will do/make

Vous ferez – You will do/make

Ils feront – They will do/make

Elles feront – They will do/make.

That's the future tense for the four most important verbs in the French language, all of which are irregular. Guess what? Do you remember the sound clue for all other French future tense constructions? It was the letter 'R'. These four most important verbs have the same R sound. Hear R at the end of a verb construction and you know you're in the future tense.

Now let's try the conditional tense for the same four verbs. Remember, it's the future stem plus the imperfect endings. Remember to look for the letter 'I' in imperfect tense endings.

Je aur<u>ais</u> – I would have (although you shorten it to J'aurais because of the vowel liaison)

Tu aur<u>ais</u> – You would have

Il aur<u>ait</u> – He would have

Elle aur<u>ait</u> – She would have

Nous aur<u>ions</u> – We would have

Vous aur<u>iez</u> – You would have

Ils aur<u>aient</u> – They would have

Elles aur<u>aient</u> – They would have.

For Être, it goes like this.

Je serais – I would be

Tu serais – You would be

Il serait – He would be

Elle serait – She would be

Nous serions – We would be

Vous seriez – You would be

Ils seraient – They would be

Elles seraient – They would be.

For Aller, it goes like this.

Je irais – I would go (although you shorten it to J'irais because of the vowel liaison)

Tu irais – you would go

Il irait – He would go

Elle irait – She would go

Nous irions – we would go

Vous iriez – You would go

Ils iraient – They would go

Elles iraient – They would go.

For Faire, it is this.

Je ferais – I would do/make

Tu ferais – You would do/make

Il ferait – He would do/make

Elle ferait – She would do/make

Nous ferions – We would do/make

Vous feriez – You would do/make

Ils feraient – They would do/make

Elles feraient – They would do/make.

The imperfect tense for these four verbs goes like this.

J'av<u>ais</u> – I had

Tu av<u>ais</u> – You had

Il av<u>ait</u> – He had

Elle av<u>ait</u> – She had

Nous av<u>ions</u> – We had

Vous av<u>iez</u> – You had

Ils av<u>aient</u> – They had

Elles av<u>aient</u> – They had.

For Être, it goes like this.

J'étais – I was

Tu étais – You were

Il était – He was

Elle était – She was

Nous étions – We were

Vous étions – You were

Ils étaient – They were

Elles étaient – They were.

Aller goes like this.

J'allais – I went or I was going

Tu allais – You went

Il allait – He went

Elle allait – She went

Nous allions – We went

Vous alliez – You went

Ils allaient – They went

Elles allaient – They went.

For Faire, it goes like this.

Je faisais – I did or I made

Tu faisait – You did/made

Il faisait – He did/made

Elle faisait – She did/made

Nous faisions – We did/made

Vous faisiez – You did/made

Ils faisaient – They did/made

Elles faisaient – They did/made.

Now you know the past, future, conditional, and imperfect tenses for the four most important verbs in the French language. This stretch of the mountain has been tough going. Give yourself a pat on the back for your efforts.

OTHER TYPES OF VERBS.

We've learned the three most important verbs, Avoir, Être, and Aller, plus the fourth most important verb, Faire. We've learned The Golden Rule which applies to ninety percent of all French verbs. So what does that leave? It leaves all the others, the last ten percent, which basically fall into three classes. The IR verbs, the RE verbs, and the OIR verbs. These are verbs that end in the letters IR, such as Finir, to finish; RE verbs such as Vendre, to sell; and OIR verbs such as Voir, to see. Luckily, once you've learned just one of each, there are patterns that you can use again and again.

Let's start with the IR verbs.

Je finis – I start

Tu finis – You start

Il finit – He starts

Elle finit – She starts

Nous finissons – We start

Vous finnissez – You start

Ils finissent – They start

Elles finnissent – They start.

Let's try Partir, to leave.

Je pars – I leave

Tu pars – You leave

Il/Elle part – He/She leaves

Nous partons – We leave

Vous partez – You leave

Ils/Elles partent – They leave.

Venir, to come.

Je viens – I come

Tu viens – You come

Il/Elle vient – He/She comes

Nous venons – We come

Vous venez – You come

Ils/Elles viennent – They come.

Notice the endings. For Je and Tu it is the letter 's'. For Il and Elle it is the letter 't'. For Nous it is 'ons'. For Vous it is 'ez'. For Ils and Elles it is 'ent'. Look familiar? By now, it should do. You're not still at Base Camp are you?

Let's look at the RE verbs.

Je vends – I sell

Tu vends – You sell

Il/Elle vend – He/She sells

Nous vendons – We sell

Vous vendez – You sell

Ils/Elles vendent – They sell.

Now Prendre, to take.

Je prends – I take

Tu prends – You take

Il/Elle prend – He/She takes

Nous prenons – We take

Vous prenez – You take

Ils/Elles prennent – They take.

How about Mettre, to put.

Je mets – I put

Tu mets – You put

Il/Elle met – He/She puts

Nous mettons – We put

Vous mettez – You put

Ils/Elles mettent – They put

This should also look familiar, with one slight exception. Je and Tu still have the 's' ending, and Nous and Vous, Ils and Elles all have their usual endings, however Il and Elle have dropped the 't' at the end. Why? For no other reason than it is redundant. The French language wants to put the 't' there, but what would it actually do? You couldn't pronounce it. Vendt would still be pronounced 'vend', and prendt would still be pronounced 'prend'. As we know, language loves a shortcut therefore, if something is completely redundant, it is dispensed with. Still, the pattern is there for all to see.

Let's try another one. It's one of my favourites: Lire, to read.

Je lis – I read

Tu lis – You read

Il/Elle lit – He/She reads

Nous lisons – We read

Vous lisez – you read

Ils/Elles lisent – They read.

Patterns everywhere you look.

Now let's try the OIR verbs like Voir, to see; Vouloir, to want; and Pouvoir, to be able.

Je voi<u>s</u> – I see

Tu voi<u>s</u> – You see

Il/Elle voi<u>t</u> – He/She sees

Nous voy<u>ons</u> – We see

Vous voy<u>ez</u> – You see

Ils/Elles voi<u>ent</u> – They see.

See the pattern ?

Vouloir, to want.

Je veux – I want

Tu veux – You want

Il/Elle veut – He/She wants

Nous voulons – We want

Vous voulez – You want

Ils/Elles veulent – They want.

Pouvoir, to be able.

Je peux – I can

Tu peux – You can

Il/Elle peut– He/She can

Nous pouvons – We can

Vous pouvez – You can

Ils/Elles peuvent – they can.

Notice how in Vouloir and Pouvoir, where you expected an 's' at the end, you got an 'x'. These are the only two instances in the French language when this occurs. It probably has something to do with pronunciation. Je veux with an 's' instead of an 'x' would sound too similar to 'vous' which would just get confusing. Rather cleverly, for these two verbs only, the 'x' ending serves as a substitute. Otherwise, look for the pattern.

Try it for Savoir, which means 'to know'.

Je sai<u>s</u> – I know

Tu sai<u>s</u> – You know

Il/Elle sai<u>t</u> – He/She knows

Nous sav<u>ons</u> – We know

Vous sav<u>ez</u> – You know

Ils/Elles sav<u>ent</u> – They know.

Is that better? Do you know where you are again? Here's another tip for you intrepid mountaineers. Just because you may be lost, don't think that your compass is broken. It's not. There are patterns everywhere you look in French.

You know how to form the past tense in French. It's a three-part structure. The first two parts come from Avoir (unless you're conjugating a verb of movement, in which case it's Être), plus the past participle. For regular ER verbs, the past participle is just the R removed and an accent aigu over the 'E', like in 'parlé'. Well, for these IR, RE, and OIR verbs, you're just going to have to learn the past participles for themselves although, as always, there are patterns everywhere.

Here's a list of some of the more important ones.

For Voir, the past participle is 'vu'.

For Pouvoir, it is 'pu'.

For Vouloir, it is 'voulu'.

For Prendre it is 'pris'.

For Mettre it is 'mis'.

For Venir it is 'venu'.

For Partir it is 'parti'.

For Finir it is 'fini'.

How do you say 'I saw' or 'I have seen'? J'ai vu.

How do you say 'You were able'? Tu as pu.

How do you say 'He wanted'? Il a voulu.

How do you say 'She took'? Elle a pris.

How do you say 'We put'? Nous avons mis.

How do you say 'You came'? Vous êtes venu. (It's a verb of movement so it uses Être instead of Avoir)

How do you say 'They left'? Ils sont parti. (Again it's a verb of movement so it's formed with Être)

How do you say 'They finished'? Elles ont fini.

Now you're speaking French. Très bien. Excellent travaille.

OTHER THINGS TO KNOW.

I studied French at school, but I never really understood it. At that age, there were lots of things to find funny about learning a foreign language. I spent too much time messing around, and I didn't learn much French. I tried again at college. I was studying an entirely different course, but within me I had this desire to learn French so I volunteered for an extra class. It was only an hour a week, so it just added to my frustration. Each week was like starting over again from scratch. Although I had the hunger, I don't think I learned much at all. And then I went to the South of France. As a life-experience, it was amazing. I spent four months there, but it was more about living than learning. At first, I promised myself that I was going to avoid English-speakers like the plague. I wanted no part of that ex-pat nonsense. I was going to live and act like a Frenchman for the duration of my stay. It was only going to be four months. I wanted to pick up as much of the language as possible in that time. Well, after two weeks on my own, I practically pounced on the next English-speaker that I came across. Loneliness defeated learning in this instance. Still, I had French telly, French radio, French shopping, French friends, all of which and whom could extend my knowledge. I had every opportunity to improve my languages skills. It was up to me how much I chose to take advantage of it.

I signed up for a month-long course at the Alliance Française language school in Nice, about a ten minute train ride from my seafront apartment in Villefranche, one of the most beautiful towns in the world. From Monday to Friday, from nine in the morning until one in the afternoon, for four whole weeks, I was taught French by a professional language tutor. It was great. The class was small. There were only six of us. One was an English bloke, similar age to myself, who had decided to emigrate with his French-speaking partner. Another was a Mexican woman with an Irish husband who had also decided to move to the South of France. (Hey, who can blame them). Another was a Hungarian barrister whose two sons were at university in Nice. She came over to visit them, and wanted to improve her French language skills and give herself something to do during the day while her boys were at uni. Then there was a young footballer from Argentina. He had been signed by the French club, Nice, and was coming up through their football academy. As part of their duty of care, they were sending him for French lessons. Finally, there was a young woman from Sweden who had come with her fiancé to live in France. It was an eclectic mix and, together with an excellent teacher called Sten Roi, we all had a lovely time. Did I learn much French? A little. It was certainly a good grounding in the language but, as with all classes, you tend to move at the pace of the slowest in the group.

Then there was university. I've covered that elsewhere. Wrong place, wrong time, and not what I would choose second time around.

Then there was night school. Yet another class. It's good practice, but you move at the pace of the slowest in the group and I'm not convinced that it is the best way to learn.

The informal French club, who used to meet each Tuesday for a couple of hours? That was good. Practice makes perfect. You've got to push yourself. Practice what you're learned. Even if you just listen in to other people's conversations (which is allowed in this environment. It's not to be recommended elsewhere!) and try to make sense of it all, it's still good learning. Try to find a French-speaker to converse with if possible. Don't be afraid to get out of your comfort zone. If you're uncomfortable, that means you're pushing yourself. Trust me, at that point, you'll be learning.

Finally, there was my year spent teaching the Beginners group everything I'd learned from all the books and CDs that I'd read and listened to over the years. Using all the tips that I'd gathered, together with all the things that I wish I'd known or ways in which I wish I had been taught. Teaching the group was great for my own learning. It reinforced, on a weekly basis, everything that I already knew, and also allowed me to move forward a little with each lesson too. It moved me up the mountain. In all, I'd say you have to take advantage of every opportunity available to you. However you're learning, whatever you're learning, you're learning. However you choose to propel yourself up the mountain, remember that no one else can do it for you. It's yours to climb, and the achievement will be all your own when you eventually get there.

LIST OF REGULAR ER VERBS.

You know The Golden rule, and you know that The Golden Rule never, ever, ever, ever changes. You learn one ER verb, for example Parler, and you use the exact same endings for every other regular ER verb. These verbs make up more than ninety percent of all the verbs in the entire French language. There are thousands of them, and you can now use them all using just The Golden Rule. Here's a list of simple ER verbs. The meaning of the ones listed below are pretty obvious. You'll recognise them straight away, and you can use them straight away, because once you can conjugate one verb, you do exactly the same for all the rest. All of them. That's The Golden Rule.

Abandonner, absorber, accompagner, accumuler, accuser, achever, acquitter, adapter, adhérer, admirer, adopter, adorer, adresser, affecter, affronter, aggraver, agréer, aider, ajourner, amuser, animer, annuler, anticiper, apaiser, approcher, argumenter, arranger, arriver, assembler, assister, attacher, attaquer, autoriser, avancer, bander, baptiser, barrer, braver, bronzer, brosser, calmer, camper, capturer, caresser, causer, céder, censurer, changer, charger, chatter, circuler, cliquer, cloner, collaborer, commander, commencer, comparer, compléter, composer, concentrer, concerner, confesser, confirmer, conformer, confronter, connecter, conserver, considérer, console, consulter, contaminer, contempler, continuer, contrôler, coopérer, coordonner, créer, crier, critiquer, cultiver, danser, décider, déclarer, décliner, dégrader, désirer, détacher, détecter, déterminer, détester, développer, disperser, dissuader, doubler, éditer, éliminer, émanciper, émigrer, employer, encourager, endurer, engager, envisager, équiper, éroder, estimer, évaluer, évaporer, évoquer, examiner, exciter, excuser, exister, expirer, exploiter, explorer, exporter, exposer, fabriquer, fasciner, forcer, fréquenter, griller, guider, hésiter, hiberner, honorer, hospitaliser, humilier, hypnotiser, identifier, ignorer, illuminer, illustrer, imaginer, imiter, immobiliser, impliquer, importer, imposer, imprégner, improviser, inaugurer, incarcérer, incinérer, inciter, incliner, incorporer, indiquer, infecter, infiltrer, influencer, informer, infuser, injecter, insister, inspecter, inspirer, installer, intégrer, intercepter, intéresser, interpréter, intimider, inventer, irriter, isoler, justifier, kidnapper, libérer, limiter, manipuler, matérialiser, méditer, mesurer, mimer, minimiser, modérer, modifier, motiver, naturaliser, naviguer, noter, objecter, observer, occuper, opérer, opposer, oppresser, organiser, paralyser, passer, payer, pénétrer, persécuter, persévérer, persuader, perturber, placer, planter, pointer, poster, pratiquer, précéder, préférer, préparer, présenter, presser, proclamer, procurer, programmer, prolonger, prononcer, proposer, prospecter, protester, provoquer, pulvériser, purger, qualifier, quitter, réaliser, rebeller, recommencer, recruter, rectifier, récupérer, réformer, regretter, relaxer, rénover, réparer, répéter, représenter, réserver, résigner, respecter, ressembler, réviser, ruminer, sanctionner, saturer, sculpter, séparer, signaler, simuler, spécifier, spéculer, stabiliser, stagner, stériliser, submerger, substituer, succéder, suffoquer, superviser, supposer, taxer, terminer, terrifier, terroriser, tester, tolérer, tourner, transformer, transplanter, traverser, trembler, troubler, unifier, user, utiliser, vaciller, varier, ventiler, vérifier, vibrer, visiter, zapper.

That is almost three hundred regular ER verbs that you already know how to use.

How do you say 'I abandon? J'abandonn<u>e</u>.

How do you say 'You cause'? Tu caus<u>es</u>.

How do you say 'He dances'? Il dans<u>e</u>.

How do you say 'She explores'? Elle explor<u>e</u>.

How do you say 'We ignore'? Nous ignorons.

How do you say 'You observe'? Vous observez.

How do you say 'They protest'? Ils protestent. (masculine)

How do you say 'They visit'? Elles visitent. (feminine)

The Golden Rule. It never, ever, ever, ever, ever, ever changes.

For the plural, 'they', the ENT on the end is silent when speaking. You pronounce it like this: ProtesT. ViseeT (in this instance). You put very strong emphasis on the last letter, with a lingering, very Gallic pronunciation. Don't be afraid to embrace your inner French person!

LEARN LIKE A KID DOES.

Children have a love of learning. They're also unafraid to make mistakes. They don't know any different. As adults and teachers, we embrace our children's thirst for knowledge. We teach them it in songs, and with games, and in the structured learning environments of nurseries and schools. They're learning from a very young age, and they're learning all the time, because everything is new to them.

That passion, plus a lifetime in which to do it, are obvious factors in a child's development. It's how we all ultimately become fluent in our native tongue. Let's face it, if we've decided to take up French at the age of thirty, forty, fifty, or sixty, we've given some of the others quite a head start. But, you can do it. With time and effort, you can climb the mountain. After all, there are plenty of older people still achieving their goals, learning languages and, yes, climbing mountains.

That said, I hope this book will inspire and help people of all ages who are serious about learning French. Starting your A-levels or about to embark on a degree at university? This is your companion piece. Tried many times and always seem to eventually drift away from it, stepping on to the mountain only to step back off again? Well if you want to get back on, take this book with you. This might just be the occasion where you finally conquer it, or at least climb higher than you've ever done before.

So what's all this stuff about learning like a kid? Remember that song 'Head and shoulders, knees and toes. Knees and toes.' You sing it to a child (it was probably sang to all of us, too, if you can remember that far back!) As you sing it, you point to all the places that you're singing about. Eventually, the message gets through. That round thing on top of my shoulders is my head. And how did I know it was resting on my shoulders? Oh, yes, because that was in the song too. What was the rest of it? 'Eyes and ears and mouth and nose. Head and shoulders, knees and toes.' The reprise at the end just reinforces our earlier learning. So simple, yet effective. Can you do the same in French? I bet you all know the word for 'head'. Tête, right. Shoulders is 'les epaules' (like epaulettes on a uniform). Knees is 'les genoux'. Toes is (I have to look this one up) 'les doigts de pied', which means fingers of the feet, because the French word for fingers is just 'les doigts' and the word for foot is 'pied'. How about the rest of it? Eyes are 'les yeux'. Ears are 'les oreilles'. Mouth is 'la bouche'. Nose is 'le nez'. Now you can sing the song in French.

And what about numbers. Do you know those? How about colours? How about shapes? How about the clothes that you're wearing? These are the basics. If you don't know them, you're going to look pretty exposed up on that mountain. Do you really think that you can reach the top without the right clothes and equipment?

Maybe you're not looking to go that high anyway. Maybe you want to speak a little French to improve your next holiday experience. Okay, let's be honest, you would quite like to impress your friends or partner and even the natives too. There's no harm in that. Maybe you just want to be able to order a meal in a restaurant, or a drink in a bar. But, wait. What if something goes wrong? What if you have an accident in your hire car, or you trip and fall, or you suddenly develop an ache that you never had before and you have to seek medical advice. You're really going to wish then that you'd put a few more hours of practice in. You'll kick yourself for not learning the three main verbs and The Golden Rule. And all the words that are contained in this book. The next chapter has one thousand French words that you already know off by heart. And the three hundred regular ER verbs I've just given you that are almost identical to their English equivalent. You were so close. You better hope that the ache you've just got is in your shoulder or your knee. At least, that way, you should have a chance. Okay, you could just point, but that's not why we're here, and who was ever impressed by someone pointing at something? So learn the basics, and the three main verbs, as well as The Golden Rule.

I have a friend called Alex. She lectures in Law. She's one smart lady. I met Alex through a group of mutual friends. A little while later, someone was talking about Alex. Now I know a couple of people called Alex. Which Alex were they talking about? French Alex, came the reply. But I didn't know a French Alex. Alex who lectures in Law, they added. Oh I know that Alex, I said, but why do you call her French Alex? Because she's French, came the reply.

I was confused. Alex wasn't French. Alex was as English as I was, and I was born in England and I've lived there all my life (apart from the four months spent living in Villefranche, of course). I asked them to explain and, guess what, Alex was French. Born there. Raised there. So what was going on? How had she managed to master every nuance of the English language, to have not a single trace of a French accent, and to be as seemingly English as I was?

Alex has two children. They're toddlers. You're at a party, and the kids are running around, playing. The next minute, they're teetering towards some hazard. 'Watch out', Alex will tell them. 'Fais attention', she will add, which is French for the same thing. She's raised them to be bilingual from the time that they were born. The kids don't know any difference. At the moment, they've got all the time in the world, plus they're at their most eager to learn. That was how Alex had been raised too. She'd been given two languages for the price of one. That's how she got to be so good. Perfect, in fact. I guess her kids will turn out exactly the same way.

Now none of us can turn the clock back, and I can only apologise if I've made that mountain seem quite high again. The thing is though, look at the key ingredients. A thirst for knowledge (which I guess you already possess, otherwise why are you reading a book called 'Serious about learning French'), and some time and effort. Like I've said, I can't climb the mountain for you, but there's nothing to stop you from doing just that.

WORDS THAT ARE THE SAME IN ENGLISH AS IN FRENCH.

The English language is apparently one of the harder ones to learn. Luckily for us, we've been learning it and using it for all of our lives, so we've mastered it, up to a point. We can all function effectively in our native tongue. The language itself is notoriously difficult for others because it is an amalgamation. Initially, the tribes of Britain spoke Celtic and other dialects. Then, because of the constant threat posed by the Picts and later the Vikings, these British tribes invited the Anglos and the Saxons onto the island to help defend the land. The Anglos and the Saxons were Europeans from the regions of southern Denmark and northern Germany. Their language was effectively that spoken by the Germans today. As a nation, we became Anglo-Saxons. The language was half native (made up of Celtic, Gaelic, etc) and half Germanic. This happened around the fifth century A.D. and for the next five hundred years, the language settled down into one recognisable tongue that we can call English. Then the French invaded. It was 1066 and all that. All of a sudden, we had a new royal household. All of the judiciary, the laws of the land, the ruling classes, were all French. They brought with them their language. They weren't going to bother learning English. Why should they? Instead, the English had to get used to the French way of speaking, French words and vocabulary. Over the next few hundred years, if you wanted to get on, you had to speak French. Eventually, this vocabulary filtered down through the classes and entered the language. Today, English is an amalgamation of old Anglo-Saxon and French. The good news is that so many of the words that we use today in English come from French. They are the same in spelling and in meaning. This means that you have access to a huge vocabulary already. For example, almost every word in English that ends in ION comes from French. There are only three exceptions in the whole language when this isn't true, so if you're trying to think of the translation for an English word that ends in ION, chances are it's going to be the same word. Looking for the French for Aberration, Action, Accusation, Addition, Admiration, Ambition, Animation, Application, Articulation, Association, Assassination, Attention, Attraction, Audition, and Aviation? The answers are Aberration, Action, Accusation, Addition, Admiration, Ambition, Animation, Application, Articulation, Association, Assassination, Attention, Attraction, Audition, and Aviation. They are all exactly the same. Same meaning, and same spelling. And that's just the A's. How about opinion, condition, and position? They're all exactly the same. Unfortunately, translation is a word that doesn't translate! It's one of the three exceptions, and the French word for 'translation' is traduction.

The others exceptions are Explanation, which in French is Explication, and Vacation, which in French is Les Vacances. I'd also be careful with Exhibition. It can mean to take all your clothes off and run around naked! If you're looking for the word for a large event, I recommend that you use Exposition instead of Exhibition, unless you really want to make an exhibition of yourself!

And it's not just words ending in ION that come from French. Words that end in ENT or ANT, in ENCE and ANCE come from French. Different, Accent, Absent, Accident, Apparent, Argument, Arrangement, and Brilliant, and lots of others. All come from

French. English words that end in TY also come from French. The only difference is TY become TE with an accent aigu over the 'e'. Beauté, Capacité, Liberté, Fraternité, Majorité, Simplicité, and many, many more.

All words that end in BLE are French. Words such as table, terrible, infallible, irresistible, and so on.

Words that end in EL and AL are French, such as liberal (libéral) and decimal (décimal), personnel (personnel) and caramel (caramel).

Words in English that end in ATE come from the French. They belong with French verbs, and the verb ending, instead of ATE will be ER, a regular ER verb. Negotiate comes from the French 'negotier'. To contemplate comes from 'contempler'. Co-operate comes from 'co-opérer'. Cultivate is from 'cultiver'.

Words that end in ADE are also derived from the French. Blockade, balustrade, palisade, escapade, and masquerade for example. Give it a try.

Words that in English end in FY also come from French, where instead of FY they will end FIER. Satisfy is satisfier. Qualify is qualifier, and so on. Also, English words that end in ARY change to AIRE in French. Contrary, military, and necessary become contraire, militaire, and necessaire in French.

Here's another tip. If you see a French word that starts with é and you don't know what it means. Replace the 'é' with an 's' and see if you can recognise the word now. It doesn't work every time, but it seems to me that lots of French words that start with é become recognisable when you change the 'é' to an 's'. Words like épice, which means spice, and étrangere, which mean stranger, and éponge, which means sponge.

The French ending 'MENT' often stands in for the English ending 'LY'. So, for 'probably', the French is probablement. For 'totally', the French is totalement. For 'seriously' it is sérieusement. For 'evidently' it's évidemment, and for 'frequently' it's 'fréquemment', and so on.

What follows is a list of words that are exactly the same in French as in English. These are just taken from a standard pocket-sized dictionary. There must be hundreds, if not thousands more words that are exactly the same in both languages. The better the dictionary, the more you will find. The words are exactly the same for the simple reason that the English language adopted these words when the Normans came to Britain. Think of it like this. The English language is the child of two parents. One is Anglo-Saxon and the other is French. No wonder the words in the following list look so familiar to us. We're all half French!

Here's the list of words that are exactly the same in English as in French.

Abandon, abattoir, abcès, abdomen, aberration, abolition, abominable, abréviation, abrupt, absence, absent, absorbant, absurde, académie, accélérateur, accent, acceptable, accident, accord, accusation, acide, acné, acoustique, acrobate, acteur, action, addition, administrateur, admirable, admiration, admissible, adulte, affluent, agresseur, agression, agriculture, air, airbag, alarme, album, algèbre, alibi, Allah, allergie, alliance, alphabet, altitude, aluminium, amateur, ambassadeur, ambition, ambulance, amphithéâtre, anatomie, angle, animal, animation, annexe, anorak, antilope, antique, antivirus, apostrophe, apparent, application, appréciable, appréhensive, aquarium, arc, arcade, architecture, archive, argument, arithmétique, arrangement, arrogance, arrogant, art, article, articulation, artiste, aspirine, assassin, association, assurance, asthme, astrologie, athlète, atlas, atmosphère, atome, attention, attitude, attraction, audible, audience, audition, auditorium, authentique, autobiographie, automatique, automobile, autopsie, avalanche, avenue, aviation, badminton, bagage, balance, ballet, banal, bandage, banquet, bar, barbecue, base, beige, Bible, biceps, bikini, bingo, biscuit, bizarre, blâme, blasphème, blazer, blond, bluff, bombe, bouquet, bowling, brigade, brillant, brochure, bronze, brunch, brutal, bulletin, bus, câble, cactus, café, cage, calibre, calorie, camera, camp, camping, canal, cancer, canoë, capable, capacité, cape, capital, caprice, Capricorne, capsule, carafe, caramel, caravane, carbone, cardigan, caresse, caricature, carnaval, cascade, casino, cassette, catastrophe, cathédrale, centre, certain, certificat, chagrin, champagne, charme, chef, chic, chimpanzé. Chocolat, cigarette, cinéma, circuit, circulation, civil, civilisation, clandestine, classe, clergé, client, climat, clown, club, cocktail, code, cognac, cohérent, coïncidence, collection, collègue, collision, colonie, coma, comédie, commerce, commission, communication, communion, communisme, compact, comparable, compatible, compatriote, compensation, compétence, compétent, compétition, complément, complet, confirmation, congestion, conscience, consécutif, conséquence, considérable, considération, constant, consultant, consultation, contact, contraceptif, contradiction, conversation, conviction, coopération, correct, correspondance, correspondent, corridor, corruption, costume, couple, coupon, courage, couscous, cousin, crabe, crampe, création, crèche, crédit, crime, cristal, crocodile, crucifix, cruel,

cube, culture, curriculum vitae, danger, date, débris, début, décent,
décimal, décisif, décision, déclaration, défense, déficit, définitif, délicat,
délinquant, déluge, demi, démon, démonstration, dense, dentiste,
département, dépendance, dépôt, dépression, description, dessert,
destination, détail, détective, dévaluation, développement, diagonal,
dialecte, dialogue, diesel, différence, différent, dimension, diplomate,
direct, direction, discrimination, discussion, dispute, dissertation,
distance, distinct, distraction, divan, divorce, docile, dock, docteur,
doctrine, document, dollar, domaine, domestique, domino, dose,
dossier, double, doute, dramatique, dune, duplex, écho, économie,
eczéma, éducation, effervescent, élection, électronique, élégance,
élégant, élément, éléphant, e-mail, empire, énergie, enthousiasme,
enveloppe, épisode, équateur, essentiel, éternel, éternité, étiquette,
évidence, évident, exact, excellent, exception, excursion, excuse,
exercice, exorbitant, exotique, expérience, expert, exploit, explosion,
expressive, expression, extrême, exubérant, façade, face, famine,
fanfare, fantastique, farce, fascination, fatigue, fax, fédéral, féminine,
ferry, fertile, fervent, festival, fiancé, fiction, fidélité, figure, film, final,
finance, fissure, fixation, flagrant, flash, flexible, fluorescent, fluide,
flute, flux, forge, fortune, fraction, fracture, fragile, fragment, friction,
front, fruit, fugitive, futile, gaffe, galant, galop, garage, général,
génération, génital, genre, géographie, géologie, germe, girafe, glucose,
golf, gouvernement, grain, grand, gratitude, grotesque, groupe, guide,
guitare, gym, hallucination, harmonie, hélicoptère, hémisphère,
héritage, héroïne, hésitant, hésitation, hiérarchie, hobby, honorable,
horizon, horizontal, horoscope, hostile, hostilité, hôtel, humble,
humilité, humour, hygiène, iceberg, identité, idiot, ignorant, illégal,
illusion, image, imagination, imbécile, imitation, immédiat, immense,

immigration, imminent, immobile, immoral, immortel, impact, impatient, impeccable, impérial, impertinent, importance, important, importation, impossible, impression, impulsion, inaccessible, inadmissible, incalculable, incapable, incident, inclination, incognito, incohérent, incompatible, incompétent, incomplète, inconcevable, inconsistant, inconsolable, incontinent, incorrect, incorrigible, indécent, indépendance, indépendant, indestructible, indication, indifférent, indigestion, indispensable, indistinct, indulgent, industrie, inestimable, inévitable, inexact, inexcusable, inexplicable, inflammable, inflation, influence, information, infraction, infrastructure, ingrédient, inhibition, , initiation, innocent, inscription, insecte, inséparable, insolent, installation, instant, instinct, institution, instruction, instrument, intact, intelligence, intelligible, intense, intention, intérim, internet, interrogation, intersection, interview, intolérable, introduction, intuition, invisible, invitation, iris, irréparable, irréprochable, irrésistible, irresponsable, jogging, journalisme, judo, jungle, justice, karaté, kayak, kilo, kit, lamentable, lampe, lanterne, Latin, latitude, laxative, légal, légende, liaison, libéral, liberté, lieutenant, ligament, limitation, lion, liquide, littérature, littéral, local, logo, lotion, loyal, lucide, lucrative, machine, magazine, magicien, magnétique, majorité, manipulation, mannequin, manœuvre, marathon, maritime, martyr, masculin, massacre, massage, match, matériel, maternel, maths, maximum, mécanisme, médecine, médiéval, médiocre, mélodie, melon, mémorable, ménopause, mental, message, méthode, militant, minorité, minute, miracle, mirage, mixture, modem, moderne, modeste, module, moment, monologue, montage, moral, morgue, morose, motel, motif, mousse, moustache, multiple, municipal, murmure, muscle, musical, musicien, nation, nature, naval, navigation, nectar, négligent, notable, note, notion, nuance, nudiste, nylon, oasis, obese, objective, objectivité, obligation, oblique, obscène, observation, obsession, obstacle, occasion, occupation, océan, officiel, olive, omelette, opaque, opéra, opération, opinion, opposition, opticien, optimisme, option, orange, orbite, organe, organisation, organisme, orientation, original, origine, ornement, oxygène, ozone, page, panache, pancréas, panorama, parachute, parade, paradis, paradoxe, paragraphe, parallèle, paraphrase, parquet, partial, participation, passage, patience, patient, patois, patron, pension, perception, percussion, perfection, permanent, permission, perspective, pertinent, pétition, philosophie, phosphorescent, physique, piano, pigeon, piloté, piquant, pirate, poème, poignant, point, poison, pole, popularité, population, porcelaine, port, portable, portion, portrait, pose, positive, position, possibilité possible, postal, poste, pot, potentiel, précaution, précédent, prédécesseur, prédilection, préface, préfecture, préférable, préfère, préférence, préjudice, prématuré, premier, prémonition, préoccupation, préparation, préposition, prescription, présence, présent, président, prestige, prétexte, préventive, prévention, primitive, prince, principal, priorité, privilège, probable, problème, productive, production, productivité, professeur, profession, profit, programme, progrès, projection, promotion, prompt, propagande, prophète, proportion, prostitution, protection, provenance, provision, prudence, prudent, pseudonyme, psychologie, public, publicité, puérile, punch, quadruple, qualification, qualité, quantité, quartz, question, quintuple, race, racial, racisme, radar, radiateur, radiation, radical, radio, rage, réaction, réalisation, réalité, récent, réception, record, rectangle, réduction, réflexion, région, regret, relative, relation, relief, religion, répercussion, répétition, reporter, représentation, répression, reprise, reproduction, reptile, république, réputation, réservation, réserve, réservoir, résidence, résistance, résolution, respect, respiration, responsabilité, responsable, ressources, restaurant, restriction, résumé, résurrection, rétrospective, réunion, révision, révolte, rhubarbe, ridicule, rigide, risible, rival, rotation, route, routine, royal, rugby, ruine, rupture, rythme, saccharine, sachet, sacrement, sacrifice, saint, salade, salon, satellite, satin, satire, satisfaction, sauce, scandale, scénario, scène, science, scooter, score, sculpture, section, sécurité, séduction, ségrégation, semestre, sensation, séparation, sermon, service, sexe, siège, signal, signature, signification, silence, silhouette, simplicité, sincère, sinistre, site, six, slogan, snob, solide, solitude, soluble, solution, souvenir, spécial, spécimen, splendide, standard, station, statue, steak, stérile, stimulant, stratégie, stress, strict, strident, structure, studio, stupide, style, subjective, substance, substitut, subterfuge, succès, succession, succulent, suffixe, suicide, super, superbe, supplément, support, supporter, suprême, surface, surplus, surveillance, susceptible, suspect, suspense, suspension, symbole, sympathie, symphonie, symptôme, synonyme, synthétique, systématique, système, table, talent, tandem, taxi, technique, technologie, tee-shirt, téléphone, télescope, télévision, tempérament, température, tenant, tennis, tension, terme, terminal, terrain, terrible, terrier, terrorisme, testament, texte, textile, texture, théâtre, thème, théologie, théorie, thérapie, thermostat, timide, tissu, toilette, tolérable, tolérant, torrent, torture, tourisme, traction, tradition, trafic, transfusion, transit, transition, transport, triangle, tribunal, tricycle, triomphe, triple, trivial, trombone, tube, tunnel, turbulent, turquoise, type, uniforme, union, unique, univers, urgent, vacant, vaccin, vagabond, vague, vain, valide, vandalisme, vanité, variable, végétation, vengeance, verbe, vérification, véritable, versatile, version, vertical, verve, vestibule, victime, vidéo, village violence, violent, violet, virile, virtuel, virus, visibilité, visible, vision, visite, visuel, vital, vitamine, vivacité, vocation, vogue, volt, volume, vote, voyage, vulnérable, wagon, watt, week-end, western, whisky, xénophobe, xylophone, yacht, zèbre, zéro, zeste, zigzag, zinc, zodiaque, zone, zoo, zoologie.

Now, most of you probably noticed that there were some subtle differences to some of the words listed above, but I'm guessing you're all intelligent enough to make the leap and, as I've said before, don't be afraid to make mistakes. We all do it, even in our first language, English, so it's perfectly acceptable to make them in French. Plus, if you've had to make an educated guess with some of the words above, that means you're doing a bit of work. Can you climb a mountain without it involving a bit of work? I don't think so. And if you can't work out the meaning of lampe, lanterne, legende, and lucide then I suggest that you give up now.

There are over one thousand words in the glossary above. That's more than one thousand words that you already have in your French vocabulary. You're well on your way to speaking French, you're climbing up the mountain, step by step. Try using some of your simple ER verbs, or your three most important verbs, together with some of the words in your new French vocabulary and see how easy it is to start forming elaborate sentences. Think you're speaking French right now? Yes, you are, you intrepid lot. Let's try some on for size.

J'admire votre ambition.

J'ai eu un bon audition.

Il a eu un mal audition.

Tu es riche.

Elle est arrogante.

Nous sommes enthousiastique.

L'évidence est inconsistent et inadmissable.

L'accusation est faux.

Mon ambition est grand.

Il aime astrologie.

Elle n'aime pas astrologie.

L'alphabet est excellent.

L'opération étais un succés !

LE and LA, TU and VOUS.

Many English speakers wonder why French nouns have a gender. What's with all the Le and La, Un and Une? We don't use them in English. Are they necessary? We could, frankly, do without them. Unfortunately, the English language is apparently unique in the world for not having either genders or classes of nouns. Because ours is an amalgamated language, we probably had so much to choose from, so much to learn, that something had to give. What we lost was accuracy. It is why speakers of other languages find English so difficult to learn. It is a fusion of Anglo, Saxon, and French. There's no real consistency to the language. Not only that, the languages that were thrown into the melting pot are all so different that the result is a bit of a monster, and yet we all still wonder why French is so hard!

Most other languages follow a more rigid structure. There is order where in English there is chaos. Bestowing gender upon nouns allows for greater accuracy because it makes the language more sophisticated. Imagine if you were talking about a group of men in English, and you wanted to say that they are going swimming. You would say 'They are going swimming'. Imagine if you were then talking about a group of women and you wanted to say that they are going swimming. You would say 'They are going swimming'. In these examples, the English 'they' could refer to either a group of men or a group of women. In French, you would either say 'Ils vont nager' or 'Elles vont nager' and a listener would immediately know if you were talking about a group of men or a group of women. Accuracy and sophistication. Every other language in the world has a method with which to do this. English does not. As English speakers, attempting to learn French, we'll just have to accept it. It makes for a bit more effort, learning the Le and the La together with the noun, but who said learning a foreign language was easy? I know that I didn't. There are some rules that give clues to whether a noun is masculine or feminine, a 'le' or a 'la'. For example, most French words ending in 'ion' are feminine. The condition will be 'la condition'. If you see a noun that ends in 'ment' it is usually masculine, so 'fragment' will be 'le fragment'. However, there are so many exceptions to all of these rules that I would suggest you would be better off just learning the gender at the same time that you learn the new word. Add both the gender and the noun to your vocabulary. There are no real shortcuts because the French language is riddled with exceptions to these gender rules.

Another strange quirk of the French language is the use of TU and VOUS. Both words means 'you'. In one sense, 'vous' is the plural, so we don't have to worry about that. If you're referring to 'you' when 'you' is more than one person, i.e. you two, then 'vous' is the correct form. If however you are talking to one person, there are rules about which form to use, 'tu' or 'vous'. Generally, if you're talking to someone that you don't know very well, if you're trying to be polite and respectful, then you use the more formal 'vous' version. If you're talking to a friend, or a child, or a family member, then you use 'tu'. I remember there was a French cop show on television. Now, when addressing a policeman, I'm sure all of us would speak respectfully and use the 'vous' form, in much the same way that you might say 'Excuse me, officer, do you have the time?', etc. In this tv show, the hardened criminals, under questioning from the police, would address them as 'tu'. This was meant to show a certain lack of respect for the officers. 'You're no better than me.' 'I don't respect you.' 'I'm going to talk down to you', that sort of thing. That, then, is the difference. TU is informal. VOUS is formal.

I remember I went to a lecture at a local library given by a guest speaker from the Alliance Française. The speaker was a lady of similar age to myself, somewhere in her forties. The subject was the French flair for resistance, such as that exhibited in the uprisings that led to the Revolution, and in the Second World War, etc. The lecture was to be followed by a question and answer session. As I listened, I psyched myself up to ask a question at the end. I thought that I could really test my French if I was able to ask something of the lecturer, if she understood me well enough to give me a reply.

The room was packed with fluent French speakers so I was a little nervous, but if I've learned one thing about learning French it is this. You have to be prepared to get out of your comfort zone. You have to make an effort, and put embarrassment aside. You have to be intrepid. Fearless, even. The mountain is nobody's living room. It can be a harsh place, and you better 'man-up' for the challenge.

My question was this. Did the lecturer think that the familiar uprisings in France, where hundreds of vehicles are regularly set ablaze, were a modern symbol of the French spirit of resistance?

Est-ce que tu pense que la situation en France dans les Banlieues, quand les voitures sont en flammé, est le meme chose de l'ésprit de la Revolution ?

Note – in France, the ghettos tend to be on the fringes of the cities, unlike in England where they tend to be close to the city centres. The French ghettos are situated in the suburbs, and the word for suburbs is les Banlieues.

Back to the lecture. Elle a repondit a moi. She answered me. I felt great.

Then, as the room emptied after the Q and A session, a man sidled up to me and admonished me for my impertinent question. I had been so busy trying to find the right words to ask my question that I had used the TU form of the verb Penser, to think, rather than the VOUS form, which was absolutely the more correct form for the situation. I was told that there had been an audible gasp in the room at my faux-pas. I had really let the side down. Well, guess what. I hadn't heard any audible gasp. The lecturer possibly indulged me a little. She probably let me off when she could have given me a disappointed look. She could even have insisted that I ask the question again, this time giving her all the respect that was due. She didn't. She let me off. She answered my question. She probably understood that I was learning. That I'd made a mistake but that I was trying to speak to her in her native language. She gave me marks for effort. And, do you know what, I asked my question and I got an answer. I was moving up the mountain. Yes, I made a mistake. Somewhere down the line (or further up the mountain) I won't make that mistake. For now, I think it's more important to keep trying. If we're aiming for perfection at the outset, I don't think any of us will ever learn French. Instead, learn like a kid does, and don't be afraid to make mistakes.

Another thing that used to confuse me was Reflexive verbs. When I first read 'noun nous levons' or 'vous vous appelez' I used to thing 'what on earth is that all about?' Basically, there are only a limited number of so-called reflexive verbs in French, although many more can become reflexive when you are doing (whatever verb you're doing) the verb to yourself, for example if you're driving yourself as opposed to driving your car, so instead of 'Je conduis ma voiture' (I am driving my car), you could say 'Je me conduis fou!' (I'm driving myself crazy!). If you want to say 'He is calling the police' it's 'Il appele la police'. If you want to say 'He is called John' it's 'Il s'appele John'. You reflect the verb back towards the subject of the sentence. Certain verbs are already reflexive, such as se cacher, to hide; se laver, to get washed; or se appeler, (or s'appeler with vowel liaison) to be called. You use them like this.

For Je, you use 'me'. For Tu, you use 'te'. For Il and Elle you use 'se'. For Nous you use 'nous'. For Vous you use 'vous'. For Ils and Elles you use 'se'. The rest of the verb is formed in exactly the same way as you would use it in its present, past, future, imperfect, or conditional form. Nothing else changes, but to use the verb in a reflexive form, i.e. to refer it back to yourself (or whoever it is you're talking about) you must include the reflexive word part.

I wash myself is Je me lave.

You drive yourself is Tu te conduis.

He calls himself is Il s'appele.

She looks at herself is Elle se regarde.

We love ourselves is Nous nous aimons.

You hide yourself is Vous vous cachez.

They detest themselves (masculine) is Ils se detestent.

They help themselves (feminine) is Elles se aident (or Elles s'aident with the vowel liaison).

That's all you need to know about reflexive verbs.

Here's a few words, too, about the imperative in French, i.e. giving orders. It's easy. Très façile. Ce n'est pas difficile.

If you want to issue a command, either to yourselves or to others, you just use the 'nous' or 'vous' form of the verb, saying the verb part without the subject part. So, for 'let's go' you would say 'Allons!' i.e. we are going. For 'go' as an order to someone else, you would say 'Allez!' i.e. you go.

How would you say 'let's sing'? Chansons. How would you tell someone else to sing? Chantez.

How would you say 'let's run'? Courrons. How would you tell someone else to run? Courrez.

How would you say 'let's dance'? Dansons. How would you tell someone else to dance? Dansez.

How would you say 'let's try'? Essayons. How would you tell someone else to try? Essayez.

Like that. Comme ça. C'est façile.

This book is by no means comprehensive. I haven't mentioned all the important joining words like then, after, during, since, tomorrow, yesterday, some, how, why, who, if, from, to, for, with, very, and so many, many more. You're just going to have to learn them all by yourself. Hopefully I've shown you the top of the mountain, or at least inspired you to go and take a look. I may have shown you a few of the paths that you may want to take, given you a few tips, a helping hand. I hope so. That was my aim. Now, though, it's over to you. Go climb the mountain, or sail your ocean, or go and learn French.

Maintenant, mes eleves, je pense que vous êtes prêt. Allez ! Tout de suite. Bon chance, et bon voyage.

LE FIN.

www.ingramcontent.com/pod-product-compliance
Lightning Source LLC
LaVergne TN
LVHW051508070426
835507LV00022B/2986